Understanding the Mass

ITS RELEVANCE TO DAILY LIFE

by CHARLES BELMONTE

SCEPTER PUBLISHERS
PRINCETON, NEW JERSEY

Nihil obstat   Msgr. Josefino Ramirez
Censor Librorum

Imprimatur   ✠ Jaime Cardinal Sin
Archbishop of Manila

The *Nihil obstat* and *Imprimatur* are a declaration that a work is considered to be free from doctrinal or moral error. It is not implied that those who have granted the *Nihil obstat* and *Imprimatur* agree with the contents, opinions, or statements expressed.

This paperbound edition published in 1997 by Scepter Publishers, Inc. Scepter Publishers, P.O. Box 1270, Princeton, NJ 08542, USA

ISBN 0–933932–89–8 paperback

Composition by Shoreline Graphics, Rockland, Maine
Printed in the United States of America

Contents

IV. LITURGY OF THE EUCHARIST
As Christ Commanded in the Upper Room

V. CONCLUDING RITE AND PERSONAL THANKSGIVING

APPENDIX

Abbreviations

DC	John Paul II, letter *Dominicae Cenae*, on the Mystery and Worship of the Eucharist, February 24, 1980.
DV	Second Vatican Council, *Dei Verbum*, Dogmatic Constitution on Divine Revelation.
GIRM	General Instruction of the Roman Missal, March 27, 1975.
GS	Second Vatican Council, *Gaudium et Spes*, Dogmatic Constitution on the Church in the Modern World.
ID	Sacred Congregation for the Sacraments and Divine Worship, instruction *Inaestimabile Donum*, on Certain Norms Concerning Worship of the Eucharistic Mystery, April 17, 1980.
ILM	Introduction to the Lectionary for Mass, January 21, 1981.
LG	Second Vatican Council, *Lumen Gentium*, Dogmatic Constitution on the Church.
MD	Pius XII, encyclical letter *Mediator Dei*, on the Sacred Liturgy, November 20, 1947.
MF	Paul VI, encyclical letter *Mysterium Fidei*, on the Holy Eucharist, September 3, 1965.
PO	Second Vatican Council, decree *Presbyterorum Ordinis*, on the Ministry and Life of Priests.
SC	Second Vatican Council, *Sacrosanctum Concilium*, Dogmatic Constitution on the Sacred Liturgy.

Preface

> We may have asked ourselves, at one time or another, how
> we can respond to the greatness of God's love. We may have
> wanted to see a program for Christian living clearly ex-
> plained. The answer is easy, and it is within reach of all the
> faithful: to participate lovingly in the Holy Mass, to learn to
> deepen our personal relationship with God in the sacrifice
> that summarizes all that Christ asks of us.
>
> —Blessed Josemaría Escrivá de Balaguer
> "The Eucharist, Mystery of Faith and Love," Homily

Years after these lines were written, the Second Vatican Council
restated solemnly the permanent doctrine of the Church: that the
celebration of the eucharistic sacrifice should be the center and culmination of the whole life of the Christian community and of every
faithful.

To achieve this goal, the Council continues, everyone should
understand well the liturgy and ceremonies of the Mass. "The
Church earnestly desires that Christ's faithful, when present at this
mystery of faith, should not be there as strangers or silent spectators;
on the contrary, through a good understanding of the rites and
prayers they should take part in the sacred action conscious of what
they are doing, with devotion and full collaboration" (*Sacrosanctum
Concilium*, no. 48).

This present work tries to make this understanding easier for the
man on the street, for the ordinary Christian who often does not
have access to more complete manuals on liturgy. It may also be useful for the priest as a means of catechetical instruction on the Mass.

Thus, the book is divided in two sections. The first is a systematic
explanation of the Mass as a whole. The second is a study of the different parts of the Mass. This is done from the viewpoints of liturgy,
history, theology, and practical piety. The liturgical notes follow
strictly the indications issued after the Second Vatican Council,

embodied in the *General Instruction of the Roman Missal* (1975), the *Introduction of the Lectionary for Mass* (1981), and related documents.

May this book help us to understand better and to love more the sacrifice of the altar. For the Mass is the path by which each of us can become "another Christ," reproducing in ourselves the sentiments which Christ had when offering himself in the sacrifice of the cross.

C. B.

PART I
THIS IS THE MASS

1. Sacrament and Sacrifice

Christ does not have to offer himself again and again, like the high priest going into the sanctuary year after year with the blood that is not his own, or else he would have had to suffer over and over again since the world began. Instead of that, he has made his appearance once and for all, now when history reached its fulfillment, to do away with sin by sacrificing himself.

In accordance with this divine will we have been sanctified by an offering made once for all, the body of Jesus Christ (Heb 9:25–26; 10:10).

Men are born to live; Christ was born to die.

He was born in Bethlehem to give his life for our salvation, in fulfillment of his priestly mission. Christ wants us to remember him for his death. He himself gave us the fitting memorial of it, to re-actualize and make present the very sacrifice of Calvary, to remind us that he died so that we may have life, so that we may be freed from the tyranny of sin. He told us the exact way he wanted us to commemorate his death, his resurrection, and his ascension to heaven.

The memorial he gave us is the Mass.

It is a mistake to think that the Mass is a memorial service like that on Memorial Day, or a sort of imitation of the Last Supper, or a collection of prayers. The Mass is not just a collection of prayers, no matter how beautiful or moving they may be. Our Lord becomes present in the Mass, doing something deeply supernatural: performing a sacrifice.

Before his passion, Jesus and the disciples were on the road to Jerusalem. This was his last journey to the city, and Jesus was walking ahead of the disciples. He took the Twelve aside and began to tell them what was going to happen to him: "Now we are going up to Jerusalem, and the Son of Man is about to be handed over to the chief priests and the scribes. They will condemn him to death and will hand him over to the pagans, who will mock him and spit at him and scourge him and put him to death; and after three days he will rise again" (Mk 10:33–34).

Jesus was going to offer his life to God as the ransom for our sins, as a gift for the others, as he was to declare in the Last Supper, "It will be given up for you." He sets the example for us, because "if life didn't have as its aim to give glory to God, it would be detestable— even more, loathsome." [1]

The disciples could not understand Jesus' demand for personal surrender to the will of God. They still conceived life as a commodity to be enjoyed in private pursuits and personal ambitions. While Jesus was talking about giving oneself to God for the others, by contrast, the disciples argued among themselves about who was to wield more power in the future kingdom.

"I have longed to eat this Passover with you before I suffer." An ardent desire filled Christ's heart: a desire to go through his passion and death and to leave a perpetual memorial of his sacrifice.

On the night of the Last Supper, Christ instituted the Mass. He offered his body and blood under the species of bread and wine to God the Father. Taking bread, Christ said, "This is my body which will be given up for you." Taking the chalice, he said, "This is the cup of my blood, the blood of the new and everlasting covenant. It will be shed for you and for all men so that sins may be forgiven."

Isaiah's prophecy fulfilled

In the book of Isaiah, the passages on the Servant of God strikingly presage and match in detail the passion and death of our Lord. We must keep in mind this prophecy of Isaiah if we want to understand well the passion of the Lord and, hence, to grasp the full content of the Mass.

A mysterious figure appears in these passages: the Servant of God. He is stricken with sufferings and rejected by all men. He takes our sins upon himself. He is humble and docile to God.

> For my part, I made no resistance,
> neither did I turn away.

---

[1] J. Escrivá de Balaguer, *The Way* (New York: Scepter, 1979), no. 783.

I offered my back to those who struck me,
my cheeks to those who tore at my beard;
I did not cover my face against insult and spittle.
Without beauty, without majesty (we saw him)
no looks to attract our eyes;
a thing despised and rejected by men,
a man of sorrows and familiar with suffering,
a man to make people screen their faces;
he was despised and we took no account of him.
And yet ours were the sufferings he bore,
ours the sorrows he carried.
But we, we thought of him as someone punished,
struck by God, and brought low.
Yet he was pierced through for our faults,
crushed for our sins.
On him lies a punishment that brings us peace,
and through his wounds we are healed.
We had all gone astray like sheep,
each taking his own way,
and God burdened him
with the sins of all of us.
Harshly dealt with, he bore it humbly,
he never opened his mouth,
like a lamb that is led to the slaughter-house,
like a sheep that is dumb before its shearers
never opening its mouth (Is 50:6; 53:2–7).

The sufferings of the Servant of God, however, are not accidental. Rather, they are the very means of accomplishing his universal mission:

And now God has spoken,
"I will make you the light of the nations
so that my salvation may reach
to the ends of the earth" (Is 49:6).

His resurrection is then announced:

God has been pleased to crush him with suffering.
If he offers his life in atonement,
he shall see his heirs, he shall have a long life
and through him what God wishes will be done.
His soul's anguish over
he shall see the light and be content.
Hence I will grant whole hordes for his tribute,
he shall divide the spoil with the mighty (Is 53:10–12).

We know that the features of this mysterious figure, foreseen and outlined by Isaiah eight hundred years before Christ, were not to be seen in any man in Israel—until Jesus Christ came and suffered. And to him alone would these words of St. Paul apply:

His state was divine,
yet he did not cling
to his equality with God
but emptied himself
to assume the condition of a slave,
and became as men are,
he was humbler yet,
even to accepting death,
death on a cross.

But God raised him high
and gave him the name
which is above all other names
so that all beings
in the heavens, on earth and in the underworld,
should bend the knee at the name of Jesus
and that every tongue should acclaim
Jesus Christ as Lord,
to the glory of God the Father (Phil 2:6–11).

Now we understand who is the Servant of God, crushed for our sins, and through whose wounds we are healed. Christ's sacrifice is the price of our liberation.

Worship: the soul of liturgy

We shall see how the Mass, in which Christ offers his life to God in a perfect act of worship, is the reenactment and re-actualization of this sacrifice of our redemption.

This worship is directed toward God the Father through Jesus Christ in the Holy Spirit. In the first place, it is directed toward the Father, who, as St. John's Gospel says, "loved the world so much that he gave his only Son, so that everyone who believes in him may not be lost but may have eternal life" (Jn 3:16).

This worship is also directed, in the Holy Spirit, to the Incarnate Son. We adore the Redeemer for his voluntary emptying of himself, accepted by the Father and glorified with the resurrection.

This worship, given therefore to the Trinity of the Father and of the Son and of the Holy Spirit, permeates the celebration of the Mass. And this worship must be prominent in all our encounters with the Blessed Sacrament, both when we visit our churches and when the sacred species are taken to the sick and administered to them.

THE WORDS of Jesus in the Last Supper, "Do this in memory of me," command the continuation of his sacrifice in every Mass celebrated anywhere in the world until the end of time. This was announced in the Old Testament by the prophet Malachi: "From the rising of the sun to its setting, my Name is great among the nations, and in every place there is sacrifice and there is offered to my Name a clean oblation" (Mal 1:1).

Therefore, in obedience to her Founder's behest, the Church prolongs the priestly mission of Jesus Christ mainly by means of the sacred *liturgy*. She does this, most of all, at the altar, where constantly the sacrifice of the cross is reenacted. Along with the Church, her divine Founder is present at every liturgical function giving fitting worship to God.

Every impulse of the human heart expresses itself naturally through the senses; and the worship of God, being the concern not merely of individuals but of the whole of mankind, must therefore be *social* as well. Hence, the liturgy always has a *social* and *external* dimension.

But the chief element of the liturgy should be *interior*. For each one of us must always live in Christ and give ourselves to him completely, so that in him, with him, and through him the heavenly Father may be duly worshiped and glorified. The sacred liturgy requires, however, that its exterior and interior elements be intimately linked with each other.[2]

Consequently, it is an error to think that the sacred liturgy of the Mass is only the outward or visible part of the divine worship, or that it is just an ornamental ceremonial with a list of laws and prescriptions according to which the ecclesiastical hierarchy orders the sacred rites to be performed.

God cannot be honored worthily unless the mind and the heart turn to him in quest of the perfect life which unites work and adoration. The liturgy—the adoration rendered to God by the Church in union with her divine Head—is the most efficacious means of achieving sanctity.[3]

Basic elements of the Mass

In the Last Supper, Jesus gave the apostles his body and blood to eat. In every Mass, Christ gives himself to us as spiritual food (Holy Communion). This is the sacrament of the Eucharist.

The Second Vatican Council confirms that Christ instituted the eucharistic sacrifice of his body and blood at the Last Supper.[4] "He did this in order to perpetuate the sacrifice of the cross throughout the centuries until he should come again, and so to entrust to his beloved Spouse, the Church, a memorial of his death and resurrection: a sacrament of love, a sign of unity, a bond of charity, a paschal banquet in which Christ is eaten, the mind is filled with grace, and a pledge of future glory is given to us."

Commenting on this text, Pope Paul VI says: "These words highlight both the sacrifice, which pertains to the essence of the Mass that is celebrated daily, and the sacrament in which those who participate in it through Holy Communion eat the flesh of Christ and drink the

[2] Pius XII, encyclical *Mediator Dei* [= MD], November 20, 1947, nos. 3, 20, 23, 24.
[3] MD, nos. 25 and 26.
[4] Second Vatican Council, Dogmatic Constitution *Sacrosanctum Concilium* [= SC], c. 2, no. 47.

blood of Christ, and thus receive grace, which is the beginning of eternal life, and the 'medicine of immortality' according to our Lord's words: 'The man who eats my flesh and drinks my blood enjoys eternal life, and I will raise him up on the last day' (Jn 6:55)." [5]

To understand the Mass well, we should keep in mind all these aspects. Sacrifice and sacrament (with its two elements of presence of Christ and spiritual nourishment for us) pertain to the same mystery and cannot be separated from one another.

The Lord is immolated in an unbloody way in the Mass, and he re-presents (makes present here and now) the sacrifice of the cross and applies its salvific power at the moment when he becomes sacramentally present through the words of Consecration. He becomes the spiritual food of the faithful, under the appearances of bread and wine. [6]

ALL THESE points should be considered, to have a complete picture of the Mass:

> The Mass is the memorial of the death and resurrection of the Lord, in which the sacrifice of the cross is perpetuated throughout the centuries.

> Christ is there—substantially present—under the forms of bread and wine.

> In the Mass, Christ the Lord, through the ministry of the priest, offers himself to God the Father and gives himself to the faithful as spiritual food. The faithful are associated with his offering.

> The Mass is an action of Christ himself and the Church.

> The Mass signifies and effects the unity of the people of God and achieves the building up of the body of Christ.

> The Mass is the summit and the source of all Christian worship and life.

---

[5] Paul VI, encyclical *Mysterium Fidei* [= MF], September 3, 1965, no. 5.
[6] MF, no. 34.

2. The Sacrament of the Eucharist

Jesus said to them: "Believe me when I tell you this; you can have no life in yourselves, unless you eat the flesh of the Son of Man, and drink his blood. The man who eats my flesh and drinks my blood enjoys eternal life" (Jn 6:53–54).

A sacrament is a sensible or material sign instituted by Christ, by which invisible grace is communicated to the soul. The Eucharist is the greatest of all sacraments. The reason is simple: The very Author of grace is *present* in it and gives himself to us in this sacrament as *spiritual food* (Holy Communion). However, this truth does not exhaust the richness of content of the Eucharist. The essential elements of the Eucharist are summarized by Pope John Paul II when he writes, "It is at one and at the same time a Sacrifice-Sacrament, a Communion-Sacrament, and a Presence-Sacrament." [1] In this chapter, we will go deeper into the last two points.

Christ is present

All the formularies of the Creed or symbols of faith confess that Jesus Christ our Lord was born of the Virgin Mary in a specific historical time. After his resurrection, he went to heaven, but he remains in the Church in a mysterious, hidden manner that is visible only with the eyes of faith.

Jesus promised the apostles, "I am with you all days, even unto the consummation of the world" (Mt 28:20), and fulfilled that promise. The disciples loved being with Jesus, talking to him, enjoying his presence. Consider, for instance, what happened one morning after the Lord's resurrection. The disciples had returned to their usual occupations, and that morning they were on lake Tiberias. After a whole night of fishing, they were coming back empty-handed. Jesus was standing on the shore, though the disciples did not recognize it

---

[1] John Paul II, *Redemptor Hominis*, March 4, 1979, no. 20.

was he. A short while later, at the bidding of Jesus, they turned their boat around, threw out their nets again, and caught so many fish, they could not haul them in. Then, immediately, the disciples recognized Jesus.

We can see in this miraculous catch of fish an allusion to the Church. She is compared to an unbreakable fishing net which becomes a divine and most effective instrument when she obeys Christ's words.

Upon reaching the shore, the disciples found Jesus beside a charcoal fire with fish cooking on it. Jesus invited them, "Come and have breakfast!" He then took the bread and gave it to them, and the same with the fish.

That was not a eucharistic celebration, of course, but it was a moment of intimacy for the Lord and his friends. That moment somehow reminds us of the Eucharist. There Christ makes us feel his presence in an ineffable way: His love becomes especially evident. The risen Christ is present among us, fishers of men, offering us his friendship, his abiding love. This love sustains our fraternity and makes us apostolically fruitful.

As Pope Paul VI points out in his encyclical *Mysterium Fidei*,[2] Christ is present in the Church in several ways:

> Christ is present in his Church when she prays, since he is the one who "prays for us and prays in us and to whom we pray: He prays for us as our priest, he prays in us as our head, he is prayed to by us as our God";[3] and he is the one who has promised, "Where two or three are gathered together in my name, I am there in the midst of them" (Mt 18:20).

> He is present in the Church as she performs her works of mercy, not just because whatever good we do to one of his least brethren we do to Christ himself,[4] but also because Christ is the one who performs these works through the

---

[2] MF, nos. 35–38.
[3] St. Augustine, *On Psalm* 85.1, PL 37:1081.
[4] See Mt 25:40.

Church and who continually helps men with his divine love.

He is present in the Church as she moves along on her pilgrimage with a longing to reach the portals of eternal life, for he dwells in our hearts through faith,[5] and instills charity in them through the Holy Spirit whom he gives to us.[6]

In still another genuine way, he is present in the Church as she preaches, since the Gospel she proclaims is the word of God, and it is only in the name of Christ, the Incarnate Word of God, and by his authority and with his help that it is preached.

He is present in the Church as she rules and governs the people of God, since her sacred power comes from Christ and since Christ, the "Shepherd of Shepherds,"[7] is present in the bishops who exercise that power, in keeping with the promise he made to the apostles.

He is present in the Church as she administers the sacraments.

Moreover, Christ is present in his Church in a still more sublime manner as she offers the sacrifice of the Mass in his name.

The divine Founder of the Church is present in the Mass both in the person of his minister and above all under the eucharistic species.

The transubstantiation

Whatever our senses perceive in the consecrated host, even with the help of scientific instruments, is always of the same sort—a quality: the whiteness of the bread, its softness, its roundness, its smell, etc. These are attributes. We call them, in the language of metaphysics, *accidents*. These are all our senses perceive. But from them, our mind

---

[5] See Eph 3:17.
[6] See Rom 5:5.
[7] St. Augustine, *On Psalm* 86.3, PL 37:1102.

discerns a deeper reality, something that underlies these qualities or accidents as their subject: the *thing* itself, which we call the *substance*.

We know, through Christ's words, that in the eucharistic species, none of the substance of the bread and wine remains. Their accidents or sensible qualities—as bread and wine—remain, though not, of course, as accidents of Christ's body and blood. They are held up solely by the will of God, who keeps them in existence, without inhering to any subject.

True, before the Consecration what we have on the altar are bread and wine; but as soon as the words of the Consecration are pronounced, the whole substance of the bread and that of the wine disappear, and they become the body and blood of Jesus Christ. This change is called *transubstantiation*. Just as the words which God spoke in the Upper Room are the same as those that the priest now pronounces, so, too, the host is the same. Christ is really present.

Real, not symbolic, presence

During our Lord's ministry at Galilee a woman with a chronic hemorrhage came from behind him stealthily and timidly, but with a great faith, to touch his cloak. She wanted to avoid embarrassing notice, for her sickness implied a legal impurity. She just touched the fringe of Jesus' outer garment and was immediately cured. Jesus turned around and looking at her said, "Courage, my daughter, your faith has saved you" (see Mt 9:20–22). The miracle was granted by Jesus not only because of the mere physical contact, but in answer to her faith, of which she had given such striking proof. The *presence* of the Lord and the *faith* of the woman performed the miracle.

> Do you see now how our faith must be? It must be humble. Who are you, and who am I, to deserve to be called in this way by Christ? Who are we, to be so close to him? As with that poor woman in the crowd, Christ has given us an opportunity. And not just to touch his garment a little, to feel for a moment the fringe, the hem of his cloak. We actually have Christ himself. He gives himself to us totally, with his body, his blood, his soul and his divinity. We eat him each day. We speak to him intimately as one does to a

father, as one speaks to Love itself. And all this is true. It is
no fantasy.[8]

Our Lord's presence in the sacrament is called "real" not to exclude
the idea that the others are "real," too, but rather to indicate presence *par excellence*, because this presence is *substantial*, and through it
Christ becomes present whole and entire, God and man. Thus, this
presence is not merely intentional (i.e., in the mind only) or virtual
(i.e., by power). And so it would be wrong for anyone to limit it to
symbolism, as if this most sacred sacrament were to consist in nothing more than an efficacious sign "of the spiritual presence of Christ
and of his intimate union with the faithful, the members of his Mystical Body." [9]

Therefore, it is not permissible:

> To concentrate on the notion of the sacramental sign as if
> the symbolism—which no one will deny is certainly present
> in the most blessed Eucharist—fully expressed and ex-
> hausted the manner of Christ's presence in this sacrament.

> To discuss the mystery of transubstantiation without men-
> tioning the marvellous conversion of the whole substance of
> the bread into the body and the whole substance of the wine
> into the blood of Christ, as if they involve nothing more than
> "transignification" or "transfinalization," as some call it.

> To propose and act upon the opinion that Christ our Lord is
> no longer present in the consecrated hosts that remain once
> the celebration of the sacrifice of the Mass has been
> completed.[10]

The Lord did not say, "This is a symbol of my body, and this is a
symbol of my blood," but rather: "*This is my body and my blood.*" [11]
"For what now lies beneath the aforementioned species is not what
was there before, but something completely different, and not just in

[8] J. Escrivá de Balaguer, *Friends of God* (London: Scepter, 1981), no. 199.
[9] Pius XII, *Humani Generis*, August 12, 1950.
[10] MF, no. 11.
[11] Theodore of Mopsuestia, *Commentary on Matthew*, c. 26; PG 66:714.

the estimation of Church belief but in reality, since once the substance or nature of the bread and wine has been changed into the body and blood of Christ, nothing remains of the bread and the wine except for the species—beneath which Christ is present whole and entire in his physical 'reality,' corporeally present, although not in the manner in which bodies are in a place." [12]

Obviously, this is not something which the Church has invented.

> We should examine in detail the words our Lord pronounced, "This is my body." The word *is* need not detain us. There are those who, bent upon escaping the plain meaning of the words used, say that the phrase really means "This represents my body." It sounds very close to desperation! No competent speaker would ever talk like that, least of all our Lord, least of all *then*. The word *this* deserves a closer look. Had he said, "Here is my body," he might have meant that, in some mysterious way, his body was there, along with the bread which seemed so plainly to be there. But since he said, *"This is my body"*—this which I am holding, this which looks like bread but is not, this which was bread before I blessed it—this is then his body. Similarly this, which was wine, which still looks like wine, is not wine. It is now his blood.
>
> Of course, if any man had said these same words before a piece of bread, that bread would have continued being so; but it was not any man who said these words. It was God who uttered these words and explicitly commanded the apostles to repeat that action for ever. [13]

Christ becomes our spiritual food

The Old Testament tells us of Elijah the prophet. As such, he was a source of discomfort for those who would not do God's will. The Queen of Israel, Jezebel, did not recognize the true God. She followed Baal, a false and nonexistent god, and his crowd of pseudo-

12 MF, no. 46.

13 Frank Sheed, *Theology for Beginners* (Ann Arbor, Mich.: Servant Books, 1981), p. 154.

prophets. The Israelites soon became unfaithful to the Covenant, turning away from God's friendship, demolishing his altars, and putting his prophets to the sword. Jezebel then threatened Elijah, who alone remained faithful to God and who denounced the sinful worshiping of Baal. Frightened, Elijah fled to save his life. He ran into the wilderness toward Mount Horeb. After a day's journey, he sat under a furze bush. "I have had enough, Lord," he said, "take my life; I am no better than my ancestors" (1 Kings 19:4). Then he fell exhausted and went to sleep.

In the same way that God did not abandon his people while they crossed the Sinai desert, neither did God forsake his prophet Elijah. An angel touched Elijah in his sleep and said, "Get up and eat." Elijah looked round, and there at his head was a bread baked in hot stones, and a jar of water. He ate and drank. His exhaustion was such that he lay down again. But the angel of the Lord came back a second time and invited him to eat again for "the journey will be too long for you." Strengthened by the food he walked for forty days and forty nights until he reached Horeb, the mountain of God. There, at the entrance of a cave, Elijah heard the voice of God as the sound of a gentle breeze. The prophet covered his face with his cloak, out of reverence.

God spoke to Elijah, comforted him, and sent him back on his mission. The whisper of a light breeze signifies that God is a spirit, who brings us peace and whose attributes are wise counsel and calm constancy. God converses intimately with us.

The food that sustained Elijah is a figure of the Eucharist, "strengthened by whose vigor," says the Council of Trent, "Christians are enabled to travel this pilgrimage of misery, and come at last to their heavenly fatherland." God gives us food and drink more precious than bread and a jar of water: his body and blood. As in the Last Supper and on Calvary, these are prepared in the sacrifice of the altar, and given to us.

THE Holy Eucharist acts in the soul in the same way that ordinary food nourishes the body. Life in the body begins with generation, and then our body grows to full maturity while we keep receiving food for our sustenance. Similarly, there is a spiritual generation into the life of grace: the sacrament of Baptism. There is growth in that life: the sacrament of Confirmation. All the while, however, we need spiritual food. In this case, our food is the Eucharist.

The external form of food is most appropriate to signify the union with Christ which is effected in this sacrament. However, there is a discrepancy in the comparison of the Eucharist with food. Whereas food is assimilated by the person fed, in the case of the Eucharist the person receiving it becomes assimilated into Christ.

The Eucharist also directs our eyes toward our last destination. The fullness of the New Covenant will reach its culmination in the new and everlasting Jerusalem, in heaven, where all the chosen ones shall be gathered in the eternal banquet.

> To communicate with the body and blood of our Lord is, in a certain sense, like loosening the bonds of earth and time, in order to be already with God in heaven, where Christ himself will wipe the tears from our eyes and where there will be no more death, nor mourning, nor cries of distress, because the old world will have passed away (cf. Rev 21:4).[14]

Mary, the first tabernacle

This same Christ present on the altar started to exist as man by being born of woman. "When the Divine Child was conceived, Mary's humanity gave him hands and feet, eyes and ears, and a body with which to suffer. Just as the petals of a rose after a dew close on the dew as if to absorb its energies, so too, Mary as the Mystical Rose closed upon him whom the Old Testament had described as a dew descending upon the earth." [15] For nine months he was cloistered in the virginal womb of Mary; and she passed into him everything that human nature demands for its growth.

> The God whom earth and sea and sky
> Adore and laud and magnify,
> Whose might they own, whose praise they tell,
> In Mary's body deigned to dwell.

14 J. Escrivá de Balaguer, *Conversations* (Princeton: Scepter, 1993), no. 113.
15 Fulton Sheen, *Life of Christ* (New York: McGraw-Hill, 1958), p. 18.

O Mother blest! the chosen shrine
Wherein the Architect divine,
Whose hand contains the earth and sky,
Vouchsafed in hidden guise to lie:

Blest in the message Gabriel brought;
Blest in the work the Spirit wrought;
Most blest, to bring to human birth
The long desired of all the earth.[16]

Since the flesh and bones of Mary were not different from those of
Jesus, how can the royal dignity of the Son be denied to the Mother?
When David was planning the Temple of Jerusalem on a scale of
magnificence becoming a god, he said, "This palace is not for man
but for Yahweh God" (1 Chr 29:1). How much more reasonable,
then, that God adorns Mary with all precious gifts so she may be a
worthy dwelling of his Son: the first tabernacle of Jesus Christ, God
and man.

When finally she did give him birth, it was as if a great ciborium
had opened, and she was holding in her hands the Guest who was
also the Host of the world, as if to say, "Behold, this is the lamb of
God; behold, this is he who takes away the sins of the world."

Mary is the creature closest to Jesus. "The piety of the Christian
people has always very rightly sensed a profound link between devotion to the Blessed Virgin and worship of the Eucharist. *Mary guides
the faithful to the Eucharist*." [17] She teaches us how to deal with her
Son when we receive him in Holy Communion.

---

[16] Venantius Fortunatus (530–609); trans. J. M. Neale; from *The Liturgy of the Hours*
(ICEL).
[17] John Paul II, *Redemptoris Mater*, March 25, 1987, no. 44.

3. The Mass as Sacrifice

> *Keep far away, then, my well beloved, from idolatry. I am speaking to you as men of good sense, weigh my words for yourselves. We have a cup that we bless; is not this cup we bless a communion with Christ's blood? Is not the bread we break a communion with Christ's body? The one bread makes us one body, though we are many in number; the same bread is shared by all. Or look at Israel, God's people by nature; do not those who eat their sacrifices associate themselves with the altar of sacrifice? I am not suggesting that anything can really be sacrificed to false god, or that a false god has any existence; I mean that when the heathen offer sacrifice they are really offering it to evil spirits and not to God at all. I have no mind to see you associating yourselves with evil spirits. To drink the Lord's cup, and yet to drink the cup of evil spirits, to share the Lord's feast, and to share the feast of evil spirits, is impossible for you (1 Cor 10:14–21).*

A sacrifice is the highest form of adoration. It is the offering of a victim to God in acknowledgment of God's supreme dominion as the Beginning and End of our entire lives. The victim or gift should be destroyed, or at least partially removed from human use, as an act of submission to the divine majesty. A sacrifice is not just an oblation; an oblation only offers something to God (as in the case of alms for the cult), but a sacrifice also immolates, or somehow destroys, what is offered.

The Last Supper—Calvary—the Holy Mass

During the Last Supper, our Lord anticipated the bloody sacrifice he would accomplish the following day on the cross once and for all for the redemption of the world.

We can reconstruct how our Lord celebrated the Last Supper observing the traditional rite of the Jewish Passover; it included the serving of four ceremonial cups of wine mixed with water.

The first cup was poured and the wine was blessed.

Then in succession the bitter herbs, the unleavened loaves, and the dipping sauce were brought in. At this moment, the treachery of Judas could have been foretold (Jn 13:26). The paschal lamb was also brought in.

The second cup was poured, and the father of the family instructed those present, especially the children, on the meaning of the feast (Ex 12:26, 13:8).

Then followed the singing of the first part of the *Hallel*, a song of praise to God made up of Psalms 113 to 118. Its first part went up to Psalm 113, verse 9, or according to some other authors, up to Psalm 114.

After the song, our Lord, departing from Jewish custom, got up, washed the disciples' feet with the "second water" intended to be used for washing the hands of the guests toward the end of the meal. Then he sat down (Jn 13:2–12). He expressed his desire (Lk 22:15ff.) to eat that Passover with them, since he would not eat any other. Meanwhile, he told the disciples that he was not to drink of the fruit of the vine any more (Lk 22:17); the hour of his passion was approaching.

Then he took bread, possibly a loaf which had to be left on the table as was customary to indicate that no more food was to be served, marking the end of the meal. He pronounced over it a "blessing" of "thanksgiving." He consecrated it, broke it, and gave it to the disciples.

Toward the end of the meal, the third cup was served; he consecrated it (Lk 22:20) and gave it to them to drink.

Once the institution of the Eucharist was over, they completed the second part of the *Hallel* (Mt 26:30). It is possible that the fourth cup was never served; it is not mentioned in the Scriptures. Afterward, they went out to Mount Olivet.

With this ceremony, our Lord anticipated in the Upper Room his own immolation and oblation which were to be accomplished on

Calvary the following day. Moreover, we shall see how Christ's sacrifice is as true and efficacious in every Mass as on Calvary. St. John Chrysostom, overcome with awe, expressed this identity in these accurate and eloquent words:

> I wish to add something that is clearly awe-inspiring, but do not be surprised or upset. What is this? It is the same offering, no matter who offers it, be it Peter or Paul. It is the same one that Christ gave to his disciples and the same one that priests now perform.[1]

IMAGINE one of those stars far from our solar system. Imagine a pulsar emitting radiomagnetic waves. This star has existed for eons, but it is only now that we start receiving its radiomagnetic waves. It takes hundreds of thousands of years for the waves to reach us. So, too, the sacrifice of the cross projects itself into the future and for all eternity. The Mass helps us to "tune in" on the merits of Christ's sacrifice and apply them to ourselves. And Christ lives on in his holy humanity and in his person.

Our Lord suffered on the cross sometime in the past, but his sacrifice is made actual at every moment of history. His sacrifice is not just something that happened two thousand years ago: It is still happening. Christ's sacrifice is not an heirloom or an antique that survives to the present: It is a drama as real now as then. As long as there are men on earth, it will go on.

Again, let us imagine, as in the novel by H. G. Wells, that a scientist has devised a "time tunnel." Going through this fantastic machine, one could become present at any place and time in the past with the flick of the dials. Let us imagine ourselves present at Calvary, seeing our Lord suffering and offering himself up for the sins of all of us. . . . Of course, this is not possible because that machine exists only in the imagination of the writer. However, the spiritual effects of this action of Christ on us are exactly the same when we attend the Mass today as they would have been, had we been present on Calvary. The redemptive love of Christ on the cross is projected through time and space and applied to us precisely in the Mass.

[1] *Homily on the Second Epistle to Timothy*, 2.4: PG 62:612.

We do not really travel back in time or get off the present moment. What happens is that the Mass incorporates us into a *present* redeeming act of Christ, which is substantially the same as the sacrifice of the cross. We use the expressions *to reenact*, *to re-actualize*, and *to make present* in this book to signify this happening.

The Mass, real sacrifice

By means of the mystery of the Eucharist, the sacrifice of the cross which was once carried out on Calvary is reenacted in wonderful fashion. It is constantly recalled in the Holy Mass, and its salvific power is applied for the forgiveness of sins we commit each day.[2]

This sacrifice of our redemption is renewed at each Mass. "As often as the sacrifice of the cross in which Christ, our Passover, has been sacrificed is celebrated on an altar, the work of our redemption is carried on."[3] The faithful gather around the priest and, together with him, join Jesus in offering himself to God the Father as on Calvary.

IN EVERY Mass, as in the Last Supper, the mystery of *transubstantiation* takes place. This occurs when the words of the Consecration are said by the priest. These words of the Last Supper and the Mass bear a clearly sacrificial character. Christ calls his body a sacrificial body and his blood, sacrificial blood. The expressions "to give up the body" and "to shed blood" are biblical sacrificial terms; they express the rendering of a true and proper sacrifice.

IN THE verses of the First Epistle to the Corinthians included at the beginning of this chapter, the Mass is set in sharp opposition to pagan sacrifices. The real presence is clearly asserted, and the comparison of the two worships highlights the sacrificial character of the Mass. For St. Paul, the Eucharist is the sacrifice of the Lord's body and blood, and is the sacrifice of Christians.

St. Paul starts by exhorting the Christians in Corinth to abstain from any manifestation of idolatry (see 1 Cor 10:14–21), specifically

---

[2] MF, no. 27.

[3] Second Vatican Council, Dogmatic Constitution *Lumen Gentium* [= LG], no. 3.

from the banquet that usually followed the pagan sacrifice (verse 14). He states the reason: A sacrifice and the banquet that follows it are closely related. To share in the banquet is, in effect, to participate in the sacrifice. St. Paul offers two examples to bring this point home:

(1) He reminds the Christians in Corinth of the sacrifices of Israel. In these, the people shared in the victim offered (v. 18) by eating a part of it.

(2) He makes clear what happens in the holy sacrifice of the Eucharist (v. 16): "The blessing-cup that we bless is a Communion with the blood of Christ, and the bread that we break is a Communion with the body of Christ." This affirmation, in this context, implies that by taking Communion we also participate in the sacrifice of Christ.

Then St. Paul considers a possible objection (v. 19): Since the god represented by the idol is not real, would it not be licit then to eat food sacrificed to the idols?

St. Paul answers that participation in such a banquet would be illicit because it means sharing in the pagan sacrifice, in union with the demons (v. 20).

St. Paul thus concludes that a Christian cannot take part in two opposed sacrifices: idolatrous sacrifices and the sacrifice of the altar (v. 21). This opposition gives evidence of the sacrificial character of the Mass.

IN THE Last Supper, Christ gave his apostles this command, "Do this in memory of me," making them priests of the New Testament. With these words Jesus meant: Do not just make a remembrance or memorial, a theatrical representation of what I have done. Rather *do this*, what I myself have done and as I have done it. Do not celebrate a new sacrifice, different or unrelated to my oblation, but offer exactly what I have offered and drink the chalice that I have drunk. In short, in the Last Supper, Christ was looking forward to the sacrifice of the cross, anticipating it, and establishing the manner of perpetuating it.

The Church continues offering the same sacrifice, but in an unbloody manner. The historical event that took place on Calvary does not repeat itself; neither is it continued in each Mass. The sacrifice of Christ is perfect and therefore does not need to be repeated. Glorious in heaven, Christ does not die again. The *presence* of the singular sacrifice of the cross is multiplied, overcoming time and space. Therefore, the Mass is not a new sacrifice, but rather the *reenactment* or *unbloody renewal* of the one supreme sacrifice of Calvary.

On the cross, he would die by the separation of his blood from his body. In the Last Supper, as happens in every Mass, Jesus Christ did not consecrate the bread and the wine together, but separately, to show forth the manner of his death by the separation of body and blood.

According to St. Gregory Nazianzen, the priest, uttering the words of Consecration, "sunders with unbloody cut the body and the blood of the Lord, using his voice as a sword." The double Consecration is necessary to represent the real separation of the body and blood of Christ which took place in the sacrifice of the cross. The sacramental mystical slaying (double Consecration), together with Christ's inward act of oblation, constitutes the essence of the sacrifice.

In the Mass, there is no new offering, but only another kind of presence of the same offering of Calvary through the ministry of the priest.

In the Last Supper, our Lord was *about to suffer*; on Calvary he was *suffering*; in every Mass he is present, *having suffered*, glorious, as he is in heaven. We do not envy the Jews and the holy women who were present on Calvary. We have the possibility of participating actively in Christ's sacrifice. Calvary is among us.

In the Cenacle, as in Calvary, the essential elements of the sacrifice are there: the slaying of the victim and the offering: *immolation* and *self-offering* to God the Father. But whereas in the old Jewish ritual the offering ought to be done by the priests, it was not necessary for the slaying to be done by them. It often was the work of the Temple servants. For it was not the slaying that made the victim sacred, but the offering. The essential thing was that the priest offer a living thing slain right there and then.

In the sacrifice of Calvary, the priest was perfect, for Christ was the priest. The victim was perfect, for he was the victim, too. He offered himself, slain. But not slain by himself. He was slain by others, slain indeed by his enemies. Christ is the unspotted Lamb. He set all men free from the slavery of sin and established the eternal alliance between creature and Creator, the New Covenant.

The sacrifice of the New Covenant

A covenant or testament is an agreement or compact—an alliance between two parties. In the Scriptures, it means an alliance between God and man. God renewed through Moses the old covenant with the people of Israel which was begun through Abraham. It was sealed with the blood of sacrificed animals, because blood was the sign of life.

While the Jews were in bondage in Egypt, they went through all sorts of sufferings; it was as if God had abandoned them. In reality, God had not forgotten the compact he had made with their fore-fathers. The sons of Israel, groaning in their slavery, cried out for help and from the depths of their slavery their cry came up to God. God heard their groaning and he called to mind his covenant with Abraham, Isaac and Jacob (Ex 2:23–24).

After the plagues, God struck the Egyptians further to prompt the deliverance of the Jews by smiting the firstborn in each Egyptian household. The Israelites were to be spared by sacrificing a lamb, and then marking their doorways with its blood. The angel of God seeing the blood would pass by. Thereafter, at every Passover, the Jews recalled and renewed their covenant with God by sacrificing a lamb. This paschal lamb of the Old Testament is the main sign or figure of the sacrifice of Christ.

Jesus instituted the Eucharist during the paschal celebration, on the eve of his death. He was bringing the paschal feast to its total fulfillment; he was renewing it and replacing it with the definitive sacrifice.

GOD GAVE his people the gift of his friendship through a solemn renewal of the compact of alliance, after having set them free from slavery in Egypt. This alliance had to last until the establishment of a New Covenant, and it had the following content:

> On the part of God, the election of Israel as a chosen people. God would make them a kingdom of priests, a consecrated

nation. This election demanded from them sanctity and fidelity to God's commandments.

On the part of Israel, unconditional acceptance of the will of God. The Jews would recognize him as the only God and would observe all the commandments the Lord had decreed.

The Jews accepted the terms of the covenant and God instructed Moses to prepare for its formal acceptance. Early in the morning, Moses built an altar at the foot of the mountain in the wilderness of Sinai. Then he directed some young Israelites to sacrifice bullocks; half of the blood Moses took up and put into basins, the other half he cast on the altar. And taking the Book of the Covenant, he read it to the people, and they said, "We will observe all that God has decreed; we will obey." Then Moses took the blood and sprinkled the people with it. "This," he said, "is the blood of the covenant that God has made with you." Moses, the mediator between God and the people, cast the blood of the same victims over the altar, the symbol of God, and over the Israelites, uniting God and people in solid communion.

THIS Old Covenant had to be replaced with a new one, as announced by the prophets: "See, the days are coming—it is God who speaks—when I will make a New Covenant with the House of Israel, but not a covenant like the one I made with their ancestors on the day I took them by the hand to bring them out of the land of Egypt. Deep within them I will plant my Law, writing it on their hearts. Then I will be their God and they shall be my people" (Jer 31:31–33). This New Covenant will be permanent: "I will conclude a covenant with you that shall last for ever" (Ezek 16:59).

In the New Testament, during the Last Supper, Jesus gave the liturgy of his death and resurrection to his disciples. He made a reference to the Sinai covenant: The New Covenant sealed with his blood was to be the eternal one. And what had only been foreshadowed had now become a reality: the communion of life between God and man. When Jesus said in the Last Supper, "This chalice is the New Covenant in my blood" (Lk 22:20), he was repeating the same words of Moses. But now it will be the new alliance which will never be broken. Those who will receive the Eucharist will become part of the new people of God. The old sacrifices offered in the Temple came to an end. The sacrifices of bullocks, goats, and lambs offered by the Jews have found completion in Christ's sacrifice.

The sacrifice of Christ and of the Church

History comprises two periods: first, the period when the sacrifice of the cross was awaited; and second, the period when the sacrifice was made and offered by Christ and his Church.

In this second period, the Church was founded by Christ in the community of those Twelve who, at the Last Supper, became partakers of the body and blood of the Lord. To the Church, his beloved Spouse, Christ entrusted the Eucharist: a memorial of his death and resurrection, a sacrament of love, a sign of unity. This is the Church governed by the successor of Peter and by the bishops in communion with him. And we receive the Eucharist from the Church Christ founded which in the Creed is professed as one, holy, catholic and apostolic.

IN THE First Epistle to the Corinthians, St. Paul explains what the Eucharist is and its origin. He says that he had not invented it, but that he had just "received" it. It all began with Christ's action "on the same night he was betrayed" (1 Cor 11:23). From Christ came the command to do this in memory of him, and in obedience to that command, we continue thanking God, breaking the bread, distributing his body, and presenting the chalice of his blood as that of the New and Everlasting Covenant.

Christ bequeathed his sacrifice to the whole Church, not just to each believer. God wants to save men, not merely as individuals without any bond or link between one another. Rather, he wants to bring men together as one people. But that bond is established when the Church celebrates the sacrifice of Christ on the cross, when she proclaims "the Lord's death until he comes," and later, when the faithful approach the sacrament of the altar.

Therefore, each Mass presupposes union among the faithful and of the faithful with their bishop, with the pope, and with the universal Church. Moreover, that solid union is made stronger with the celebration of the Eucharist and is a consequence of it. The Second Vatican Council states it in this manner: "In the sacrament of the eucharistic bread, the unity of believers, who form one body in Christ, is both expressed and brought about." [4]

The Eucharist is a common possession of the Church as the sacrament of her unity. Thus, the Church has the strict duty to specify everything which concerns participation in this sacrament and its celebration.

The priest and victim

Jesus Christ is always the principal and sovereign Priest. From him did the apostles and their successors in the priesthood receive the power to celebrate the eucharistic sacrifice in his name and on behalf of the entire Church. Therefore, following Christ's command, the priest offers the Mass acting as the representative of Christ. That is why he does not say, "This is the body and blood of Christ," but, "This is my body" and "This is my blood." The priest is the chosen instrument of Christ in the same manner that the brush is the painter's tool.

Both on the cross and in the Mass, the priest and victim are one and the same: Christ himself. He is both *the one who offers* and *the one who is offered*.

In the Mass, Christ is no longer alone on the cross. Like any other sacrament, the Mass is an action of Christ and also of the Church. The Church does not offer a sacrifice different from that of Christ. At the moment of the offertory, the entire Church, hierarchically structured, presents itself for sacrifice with Christ. Christ is the only Priest and Victim, and the entire Church participates in this double role.

Thus, the sacrifice of the Mass is an act of the whole Christ, Head and members. On the part of Jesus, the surrender of self is real and perfect. It is real also on the part of those who are in the state of grace and are actually united with Christ by charity. As regards the individual Christian, the surrender of self will be real in the measure in which he really shares the dispositions of heart—absolute submission

---

[4] LG, no. 3; see also 1 Cor 10:17.

to the will of God—which are found in Jesus' heart. Sin and attachment to sin are the obstacles to sanctity. At Mass we should profess our desire to struggle to overcome these obstacles.

WHEN THE faithful are said to offer the Mass together with the priest, this does not mean that all the members of the Church celebrate the Mass like the priest himself. This is done only by the celebrant, who alone possesses the *ministerial priesthood*. He has been divinely appointed for this purpose through the sacrament of Holy Orders.

However, "the priest cannot consider himself a 'proprietor' who can make free use of the liturgical text and of the sacred rite as if it were his property, in such a way as to stamp it with his own arbitrary personal style. At times this way of doing things might seem more effective, and it may better correspond to subjective piety; nevertheless, objectively, it is always a betrayal of that union which should find its proper expression in the sacrament of unity.

"Every priest who offers the holy sacrifice should recall that during this sacrifice it is not *only* he with his community that is praying but the whole Church, which is thus expressing in this sacrament her spiritual unity, among other ways by the *use of the approved liturgical text*." 5

The faithful are said to offer the Mass with the priest when they unite their praise, petition, expiation, and thanksgiving with the prayer of the priest, indeed, with the prayer of Christ himself. In doing so, the faithful exercise some element of Christ's priesthood which is imparted to them at baptism. This participation in Christ's priesthood is called common priesthood. All these intentions are presented to God the Father by means of the priest's external rite.

United with Christ and Mary

The principal Victim of the sacrifice, then, is Jesus Christ, but the faithful, in order to exercise their *common priesthood* fully, should unite their sacrifice to his and thus offer themselves also to God the Father. "I exhort you . . . to present your bodies as a sacrifice, living, holy, pleasing to God, your spiritual service," wrote St. Paul to the Romans (12:1).

5 John Paul II, letter *Dominicae Cenae* [= DC], February 24, 1980, no. 12.

The Mass requires all Christians, so far as human power allows, to reproduce in themselves the sentiments that Christ had when he was offering himself in sacrifice: sentiments of humility, of adoration, praise and thanksgiving to the divine Majesty. It requires them also to become victims, as it were; cultivating a spirit of self-denial according to the precepts of the Gospel, willingly doing works of penance, detesting and expiating for their sins. It requires all of us, in a word, to die mystically with Jesus Christ on the cross, so that we may say with the same apostle, "With Christ, I hang upon the cross." [6]

The unity of believers centered on the Eucharist is one clear precept of Christ. The disciples of Jesus faithfully executed this command, persevering in prayer and assembling to celebrate the eucharistic sacrifice, together with Mary, the Mother of Jesus, all having but one heart and one soul.

Mary's participation in Christ's sacrifice is unique. Standing at the foot of the cross, she actively cooperated with the redemption accomplished by her Son. She stood "suffering deeply with her only-begotten Son and joining herself with her maternal spirit to his sacrifice, lovingly consenting to the immolation of the Victim to whom she had given birth; in this way Mary faithfully preserved her union with her Son even to the cross." [7] She was associated with Christ in the sacrifice of the cross, and the same sacrifice is reenacted in every Mass. Thus, Mary is present in a mystical manner in every Mass.

The Sunday Precept

The third commandment of the Decalogue states: "Remember to keep holy the Lord's day." It commands us to honor God with acts of worship on prescribed days.

In the Old Testament, God commanded the chosen people to keep holy the Sabbath day (Saturday). This precept reminded them that God rested from his work of creation upon its completion on the seventh day, and that God blessed and sanctified that day (Ger 2:2–3).

---

[6] MD, no. 125.
[7] LG, no. 58.

In the New Testament, Sunday is the Lord's day (*dies dominica*). On that day we celebrate the new creation—the re-creation—of man as a son of God by grace. The beginning of man's birth to the life of grace, the Lord's resurrection, was on such a day. This supernatural new creation is far superior to the material creation of the world.

To assure and facilitate the proper sanctification of Sundays and other chief feasts, the Church prescribes attendance at Holy Mass during these days. This is prescribed in the Church's first commandment. The precept to attend Holy Mass obliges us to hear a complete Mass either on the same Sunday (or holy day) or in the afternoon of the previous day. Attending a complete Mass entails following at least its essential parts with bodily presence and pious attention.

The correct and pious observance of the first precept of the Church guarantees the fulfillment of God's third commandment.

WE HAVE testimonies from the very beginning of the life of the Church which prove that the Christians celebrated the Holy Mass especially on Sunday, the day the Lord triumphed by rising from the dead.

We read in the Acts of the Apostles (20:7–12): "On the first day of the week we met to break bread." The verb used for "meeting" has for its noun *synaxis*, the Greek for Eucharist.

The Second Vatican Council offers us a deep theological explanation of the Sunday precept: "By tradition handed down from the apostles which took its origin from the very day of Christ's resurrection, the Church celebrates the paschal mystery every eighth day; with good reason this, then, bears the name of the Lord's day or Sunday. For on this day Christ's faithful should come together into one place so that, by hearing the word of God and taking part in the Eucharist, they may call to mind the passion, the resurrection, and the glorification of the Lord Jesus, and may thank God who has begotten them again, through the resurrection of Jesus Christ from the dead, unto a living hope (1 Pet 1:3)." [8]

No wonder, then, that the Church requires us to go to Mass at least on Sunday under the pain of mortal sin.

[8] SC, no. 106.

4. The Mass in the Life of Each Christian

Until the Lord comes, therefore, every time you eat this bread and drink this cup, you are proclaiming his death, and so anyone who eats the bread and drinks the cup of the Lord unworthily will be behaving unworthily toward the body and blood of the Lord (1 Cor 11:26–27).

Since you have been brought back to true life with Christ, you must look for the things that are in heaven, where Christ is, sitting at God's right hand (Col 3:1).

The sacrifice that Jesus offered on the cross accomplished three things:

It atoned for the sin of the human race.
It healed the breach between men and God.
It opened heaven to man.

Is there still something left to be done? Yes, but what remains is not an addition to what was done on Calvary, but the application to each man of the merits of Christ.

Every human being was redeemed on the cross by Christ (*objective redemption*); it is up to each to apply to himself this redemption freely and cooperate with grace (*subjective redemption*).

The passion and death of Christ, the unique sacrifice that took away our sins, is indeed a life-giving remedy. But it can be compared to a medicine, which, thoroughly efficacious in itself, benefits only those who actually apply it. The New Covenant is not unilateral. God, who procured the means of salvation for one and all, requires our own cooperation. Each of us should receive for himself what our Lord won—through his cross—for mankind. We cooperate by receiving the sacraments, especially the Holy Eucharist; by prayer, penance, and by leading a Christian life; by corresponding to the graces God sends us.

Since the Mass is the same sacrifice as that of Calvary with all its strength and sanctifying power, the Church considers it the center of her life and the life of each child of hers who struggles, with the help of God's grace. "The eucharistic sacrifice is the 'source and summit of all Christian life.' It is a single sacrifice that embraces everything. It is the greatest treasure of the Church. It is her life." [1]

St. Augustine tells us a similar idea: "He who wants to live can find here a place to live in and the means to live on. Let him approach, let him be incorporated so that he may receive life. Let him not shy away from union with the members, let him not be a rotten member that deserves to be cut away, nor a distorted member to be ashamed of: let him be beautiful, let him be fitting, let him be healthy. Let him adhere to the body: let him live for God on God: let him labor now upon earth, so that he may afterward reign in heaven." [2]

The Church strongly recommends all the faithful to participate often in the Mass. "The more perfect form of participation in the Mass whereby the faithful, after the priest's Communion, receive the Lord's body from the same sacrifice is warmly recommended to those who are duly prepared and in the state of grace." [3]

The wedding garment

Our Lord said that the kingdom of heaven is like a king who held a marriage feast for his son. He sent his servants to call in those invited to the marriage feast, but they would not come. Again he sent out other servants to invite the people, but they paid no attention to them. So the king punished those people. Then the king told his servants to gather all whom they could find and bring them to the marriage feast, because everything was ready.

The king went in to see the guests. He saw there a man who had not put on a wedding garment, and he said to him, "How did you get in here, my friend, without a wedding garment?" The man did not know what to say. So the king said to his servants, "Bind him

---

[1] John Paul II, "Prayer on Holy Thursday" (1982).
[2] St. Augustine, *Treatise on John* 26.13; PL 35:1613.
[3] SC, no. 55.

hand and foot and throw him out into the dark, where there will be weeping and grinding of teeth" (Mt 22:1–14).

The king in this parable is, of course, God the Father; Jesus is the son whose marriage feast is held; he is wedded to his Church. The marriage feast is specifically the sacrament of the Holy Eucharist, in which we receive him as food for our souls; thereby we remain closely united to him as members of his Church. We are invited to receive Holy Communion, but we must don a wedding garment— that is, we must be in the state of grace.

To be in the state of grace means that we must always be free from mortal sin when receiving Communion. So long as a person is not certain of having committed a mortal sin since the last confession, one is worthy to go to Communion. But if anyone receives this sacrament in a state of mortal sin, he commits a grievous sin called sacrilege.

IF ONE has committed a mortal sin, it is not enough to make an act of perfect contrition before receiving Holy Communion. It is true that an act of perfect contrition (sorrow for sin out of love for God) restores the soul to the state of grace. But how can one be sure that his act of contrition is perfect? Or that his love of God is absolute? To protect everyone against the danger of self-deception in this matter, and to protect the Holy Eucharist against the danger of profanation, the law of the Church explicitly requires that if anyone knows for sure he has committed a mortal sin, he must go to the sacrament of Penance before receiving Holy Communion.[4] This law is always binding even though one may be quite sure that he has perfect contrition for the sin.

Frequent Communion

"The Council of Trent calls the Eucharist the antidote whereby we may be freed from daily faults and be preserved from mortal sins.[5] It is desirable to have the faithful in large numbers take an active part in the sacrifice of the Mass each and every day and receive the nourish-

---

[4] Council of Trent, sess. 13, ch. 7 and c. 11.
[5] Session 13, c. 2.

ment of Holy Communion with a pure and holy mind and offer fitting thanks to Christ the Lord for such a great gift. They should remember these words of St. Pius X: 'The desire of Jesus Christ and of the Church to see all the faithful approach the sacred banquet each and every day is based on a wish to have them all united to God through the sacrament and to have them draw from it the strength to master their passions, to wash away the lesser sins that are committed every day and to prevent the serious sins to which human frailty is subject.' And they should not forget about paying a visit during the day to the most Blessed Sacrament in the very special place of honor where it is reserved in churches in keeping with the liturgical laws, since this is a proof of gratitude and a pledge of love and a display of the adoration that is owed to Christ the Lord who is present there." [6] This way Holy Communion becomes a pledge of our future immortality, an anticipation of the blissful company of God in heaven to which we all look forward.

The Mass is also the center of the life and mission of each priest, who finds in it the direction and the goal of his ministry.

Learning to appreciate the Mass

To celebrate and to offer the Holy Mass with greater fruit, we should consider that:

> The Mass is the most important event which happens to mankind each day.

> The Mass is the center of Christian life. All the sacraments, prayers, visits to the Blessed Sacrament, spiritual communions, devotions, and mortifications offered to God have the Mass as their central point of reference. If the center were to disappear (e.g., if attendance at Mass were to be consciously abandoned), then the whole Christian life would collapse.

> Even our concern for the others, our apostolate, should take its root in the Mass. "The devotion to the divine Eucharist exerts a great

---

[6] MF, no. 66; quotation from St. Pius X, decree *Sacra Tridentina Synodus*, December 20, 1905.

influence upon the soul in the direction of fostering a 'social' love, in which we put the common good ahead of private good, take up the cause of the community, the parish, the universal Church, and extend our charity to the whole world because we know that there are members of Christ everywhere." [7]

The Mass is the most pleasing offering we can make to God. Every member of the Mystical Body of Christ receives at baptism the right and duty of taking part in the sacrifice of the Head of that Body. Our Mother the Church wants us to attend Mass, not as strangers or as passive spectators, but as exerting effort to understand it better each time. We must participate in the Mass in a conscious, pious, and active manner, with the right dispositions and cooperating with divine grace. Our participation must be both *internal* and *external*.

Internal participation

Since the sacrifice of the Mass is the same as the sacrifice of Calvary, they have the same fourfold purpose:

To adore the Blessed Trinity. The sacrifice of the cross was first of all a sacrifice of adoration and praise of God. Although the Mass is sometimes offered "in honor and in memory of the saints, the Church teaches us that the Mass is not offered to the saints but to God alone who has given them their crown."

To give thanks for the many benefits we receive from God, including those which we are not aware of. Only Christ our Lord can offer God a worthy hymn of thanksgiving. He did so when he gave thanks in the Last Supper and when, hanging on the cross, he continued to give thanks. Our Lord continues to thank God the Father for us in the holy sacrifice of the Mass.

To ask pardon for our sins and for the many times we have not loved God as we should. This desire for expiation and atone-

[7] MF, no. 69.

ment should lead us to make a good confession. The same Christ who died on the cross for our sins is present and offered in the Mass "so that sins may be forgiven."

To ask for the many things, spiritual and material, which we need. The fourth purpose of the Mass is petition. Jesus Christ on the cross died "offering prayers and supplications and was heard because of his reverent obedience" and now in heaven "lives always to make intercession for us" (Heb 5:7 and 7:25). These graces benefit those who attend Holy Mass and the persons for whom it is offered.

These should be our thoughts and intentions at every Mass that we attend, uniting ourselves with Christ and making his desires and sentiments on the cross our own.

External participation

Since each of us has a soul and a body, we should participate in the Mass also externally, taking care of little details:

Attend the Mass with a spirit of prayer, praying as the Church teaches us to pray, avoiding distractions. Be one with the words, actions, and gestures of the celebrant, who acts in the person of Christ. Give up personal preferences; accept the option which the pastor, considering the circumstances of the people in each community, has chosen from among the legitimate possibilities that the liturgy offers us.

Listen, answer, acclaim, sing, or keep opportune silence in order to facilitate union with God and to deepen our reflection on the word of God. All the faithful present, whether clergy or laity, participate together, each in his own way.

Stand, sit, and kneel with the congregation, and be serene when you see someone who does not do so.

Be punctual. This is a considerate detail for Christ our Lord himself and for the others who are attending the Mass. Arrive before the priest goes to the altar. Leave only after the priest has left.

Dress properly. We should go to Mass dressed and groomed as for an important meeting and not, for instance, as if we are going to play sports.

Suggestions for a worthier participation

These ideas may help you to participate better in the Holy Mass:

Pray on the way to Mass. Whether you drive to a distant chapel or walk down the street to a cathedral, turn your attention to the coming celebration. Prepare your soul for Communion with acts of love of God. Make acts of contrition and atonement to make up to the Lord for past failures. Pray for the priest so that he may truly minister to the needs of the parish. Pray for the congregation so that they may open their minds and hearts to what will be taught them, and pray that you may understand what you yourself will be taught at Mass.

Use your missal, if you have one, or the missalette available in the church. By reading and following the prayers of the priest, you can avoid distractions.

The missalettes for the use of the faithful usually contain the variable prayers for each day's Mass and most of the fixed parts of the Order of Mass arranged in their usual sequence.

The more complete missals for the faithful have the prayers of the Mass distributed in three main sections. You should mark them before the Mass starts:

- The *Ordinary of the Mass* or fixed prayers of the *Order of Mass*. These include, among others, the Penitential Rite, the Kyrie, the Gloria, the Creed, the Preparation of the Gifts, the Eucharistic Prayers, the Lord's Prayer, the Rite of Peace, the Agnus Dei, and the Concluding Rite.
- *Proper Prayers*, variable for each day's Mass. These include the Entrance Antiphon, the Presidential Prayers (the Opening Prayer or Collect, the Prayer over the Gifts, and the Prayer after Communion), and the Communion Antiphon.
- *Readings*. This section includes the First Reading, the Responsorial Psalm, the Second Reading (when there is

one), the Gospel Acclamation (or *Alleluia*), and the Gospel.

Offer this sublime sacrifice in union with the Church. Live the Holy Mass, feeling yourself to be part of the Church, the Mystical Body of Christ, the people of God. Be united to the bishop of the diocese where the Mass is being offered and to the pope, the Vicar of Christ for the universal Church.

Be united to the sacrifice of Jesus, who is the only Victim. By doing so, you also offer to God the Father through Christ, and with the Holy Spirit, all the sacrifices, sufferings, self-denials, and tribulations of each day.

Have the necessary preparation for Communion. If you are going to receive Holy Communion, you need—besides being in the state of grace—to have the right intention and keep the eucharistic fast.

- The *right intention* in receiving Communion means having this good purpose: to please God, to achieve greater union with him through charity, and to apply this divine remedy to one's moral weaknesses. The sacrament should not be received out of routine, vainglory, or human respect.
- The *eucharistic fast* requires abstaining from eating and drinking, except water and medicine, for one hour before actual Communion time. The sick and the elderly, as well as those who take care of them, may receive Holy Communion even if they have taken something within the hour.
- We are bound to receive Holy Communion, under serious obligation, at least once a year—ordinarily in Easter time—and when we are in danger of death.
- Holy Communion may be received a second time on the same day when one attends Holy Mass again on that day, and when one receives the Blessed Sacrament as viaticum in danger of death.

Complete the Mass with an intense thanksgiving. Devote a few minutes to private prayer. In this way, your Mass will have direct influence on your work, your family life, your dealings with others, and the manner you will spend the rest of your day. In short, the Mass should not be an isolated event of the day; rather, it should be the inspiration and the dynamo of all your actions.

Turn the whole day into a continuous preparation for the holy sacrifice by working and praying, by making spiritual communions, and, at the same time, into a never-ending act of thanksgiving. For a Christian, all honest activities can be turned into prayer.

Imitate the piety of the Blessed Virgin and ask her for it. While our Lord offered and immolated his flesh, Mary offered and immolated her spirit. Participate in each Mass as if it were your last.

The teaching of the Sacred Scriptures

This is a summary of the main passages of the Sacred Scriptures referring to the sacrament of the Eucharist and the Holy Mass. Your personal meditation on these passages will help you to increase your faith in this sublime mystery.

1. *Remote preparation in the Old Testament*
    The offering of Melchizedek: Gen 14:18–20.
    The sacrifice of the Covenant on the mountain of Sinai: Ex 24:3–8.
    The manna in the desert: Ex 16:2–4; cf. Jn 6:31–59.
    Elijah strengthened by bread from heaven: 1 Kings 19:4–8.
    The banquet of Wisdom: Prov 9:1–6.
    The prophecy of Malachi: Mal 1:11.
    The paschal lamb: Ex 12:1; cf. Jn 1:29, 1 Cor 5:7.
    The Servant of God: Is 42:1–7; 49:1–19; 50:4–9; 52:13–53:12.

2. *The announcing of the Eucharist*
    The miracle at Cana: Jn 2:1–12.
    The multiplication of the loaves: Lk 9:11–17; Mt 14:13–21; Jn 6:1–15.
    The parable of the wedding feast: Mt 22:1–14.
    The discourse on the bread of life: Jn 6:24–69.

3. *The institution of the Eucharist*
    St. Paul's narrative: 1 Cor 11:23–26.
    St. Luke's narrative: Lk 22:14–20.
    St. Matthew's narrative: Mt 26:26–29.
    St. Mark's narrative: Mk 14:22–25.
    Evocation of St. John: Jn 13:1–35.

4. *The meals with the risen Christ*
    On Easter Sunday with the disciples of Emmaus: Lk 24:13–35.
    The appearance to the apostles: Lk 24:41–43.
    The appearance on the shore of Tiberias: Jn 21:1–14.
    The appearance on Ascension Day: Acts 1:4.

5. *The Eucharist in the life of the early Church*
    The Breaking of the Bread at Jerusalem: Acts 2:42–47.
    The Breaking of the Bread at Troas: Acts 20:7–11.
    The sign of unity: 1 Cor 10:16–17.
    The wedding feast of the Lamb: Rev 19:9.

PART II
INTRODUCTORY RITES

The introductory rites have a twofold purpose: to make the faithful coming together take on the form of a community, and to help them prepare themselves to listen to God's word and celebrate the Eucharist properly.[1] These parts, therefore, are like an introduction to or preparation for the sacred action, integrated by the following elements:

Entrance
Veneration of the Altar
Greeting of the Congregation
Penitential Rite
The *Kyrie*
The *Gloria*
Opening Prayer or Collect

---

[1] General Instruction of the Roman Missal [= GIRM], March 27, 1975, no. 24.

5. Entrance

The bridegroom is here! Go out and meet him (Mt 25:6).

The celebration of the Mass begins with the entrance of the priest and ministers. This procession toward the altar symbolizes the journey of the pilgrim Church toward heaven. The symbolism is still clearer when the cross and the Book of the Gospels are brought: Christ, Redeemer and Teacher, assures us a safe arrival. The standing attitude of the faithful manifests both respect for the priest, as the minister of Christ, and the desire to participate in the celebration.

Let us reconstruct one of the Sunday gatherings of the fifth or sixth century in Rome. The people have taken their places in the church. The service is about to begin. The door of the *secretarium* (which adjoins the church and where the Roman pontiff and his suite vest themselves) is opened. The procession moves down the nave, while the *schola* sings the psalm of entry: the *Introit*. The pontiff is preceded by a solemn cortege of his attendant clergy, deacons, and acolytes. A subdeacon walks at the head of the procession, swinging the censer. Then, in front of the celebrant and the deacons, come seven acolytes, each holding lighted candles. These seven flames are a reminder of the visions of St. John recorded in Revelation, in which the apostle calls Christ "he who walks amidst the seven golden candlesticks" (Rev 1:12–13 and 2:1). A young cleric reverently carries the Book of the Gospels, which is placed on the altar.

Psalms are chanted by alternating choirs—in antiphonal style, as it is called. These psalms are specially chosen for their consonance with the underlying intention of the day's Mass. They are joyous in Advent; on a saint's day they hymn his glorious triumph; and when the Epiphany and the Transfiguration are being commemorated, their theme is the royalty of Christ—and so on. This was how the Introit became an entrance song or introduction.

In our time, there is but a vestige of this impressive rite; by a few brief words, the entrance song states the theme or point of emphasis of the Mass formulary which it opens. It intensifies the unity of the gathered people, leads our thoughts to the mystery of the season or feast, and accompanies the procession of the priest and ministers.[1]

In Masses with a congregation, the priest and ministers may go to the altar in this order:

a server with a lighted censer
two servers with lighted candles
and between them a server carrying the cross
other ministers
a reader with the Book of the Gospels[2]
the priest

During the procession to the altar the entrance song is sung. The antiphon and psalm of the *Graduale Romanum*—or another song—suited to this part of the Mass, the day, or the season and having a text approved by the conference of bishops, may also be used.

If there is no singing for the entrance, the antiphon in the missal is recited either by the faithful, by some of them, or by a reader; otherwise it is recited by the priest after the greeting.[3]

"Behold, the bridegroom is here! Go out to meet him" (Mt 25:6). Like the wise virgins of the parable, we seem to hear that shout when the first notes or words of the entrance song reach our ears. It is time for us to get our lamps and go out to meet the One who is coming. Thus, we will not end up having to hear that fateful "I do not recognize you" (Mt 25:12).

"Trusting firmly in God's grace, we are ready from this very moment to be generous and courageous, and take loving care of little things: we are ready to go and meet our Lord, with our lamps burning brightly. For the feast of feasts awaits us in heaven. 'Dearly beloved brethren, it is we who are called to take part in the wedding feast of the Word, we who already have faith in the Church, who are nourished on sacred Scripture, and who rejoice because the Church is united to God. Ask yourselves now, I pray you, whether you have come to the feast wearing your wedding garment: examine your

---

[1] GIRM, no. 25.

[2] Now the Book of the Gospels is usually carried by the deacon, either in front of his chest (the Roman way) or raised over his head (the Byzantine way).

[3] GIRM, no. 26.

thoughts attentively.' [4] I assure you, and I say the same to myself, that our wedding garment has to be woven with our love of God, a love we will have learnt to reap even in the most trivial things we do. It is precisely those who are in love who pay attention to details, even when they are doing apparently unimportant things." [5]

CHRIST is coming to us. He stands at the door and knocks. "Hear his knock, listen to him asking to enter, 'Open to me . . . , for my head is covered with dew, and my hair with the moisture of the night.'

> When does God the Son most often knock at your door?—
> When his head is covered with the dew of the night. He vis-
> its in love those in trouble and temptation, to save them
> from being overwhelmed by their trials. His head is covered
> with dew or moisture when those who are his body are in
> distress. That is the time when you must keep watch so that
> when the bridegroom comes he may not find himself shut
> out, and take his departure. If you were to sleep, if your
> heart were not wide awake, he would not knock but go
> away; but if your heart is watchful, he knocks and asks you
> to open the door for him.
>
> Our soul has a door; it has gates. "Lift up your heads, O
> gates, and be lifted up, eternal gates, and the King of glory
> will enter." If you open the gates of your faith, the King of
> glory will enter your house in the triumphal procession in
> honor of his passion. [6]

From the beginning of this Mass, we would like to remove the obstacle of our pride and lack of faith.

IN THE Middle Ages, the priest went to the altar reciting Psalm 43. This psalm was retained in the missal of St. Pius V. It prepared the priest, and all of us, for the celebration: "Why should I go mourning, oppressed by the foe? I will come to the altar of God, the God of my joy!" (Ps 43:2, 4).

[4] St. Gregory the Great, *Homiliae in Evangelia*, 38.11: PL 76:1289.
[5] J. Escrivá de Balaguer, *Friends of God*, no. 41.
[6] St. Ambrose, *Exposition of Psalm* 118, CSEL 62:258–259.

"No one is shut out from this joy: all share the same reason for rejoicing. Our Lord, victor over sin and death, finding no man free from sin, came to free us all. Let the saint rejoice as he sees the palm of victory at hand. Let the sinner be glad as he is being offered his forgiveness. Let the pagan take courage as he is summoned to life." [7]

We remember now the promise of our Lord: "Where two or three are gathered together in my name, I am there in the midst of them" (Mt 18:20). We contemplate the priest going toward the altar, and we see Christ in him, entering his holy Church to incorporate her in his redeeming action, the sacrifice of the altar. Yes, we should be filled with joy because Christ, in the person of the celebrant, appears among us to lead us to the spring of living waters that flow continually to bring us everlasting life. [8]

Christ is going to offer the sacrifice, and he is also the Victim to be offered. We receive him with joy because he is the spotless Lamb. We want to follow him and, with him, to offer ourselves to the Father.

[7] St. Leo the Great, *Sermo* 1 *in Nativitate Domini*.
[8] See Jn 4:14.

6. Veneration of the Altar and Greeting of the Congregation

The grace of the Lord Jesus Christ, the love of God and the fellow-ship of the Holy Spirit be with you all (2 Cor 13:13).

On reaching the altar, the priest and ministers make the proper reverence—that is, a low bow or a genuflection, if there is a tabernacle containing the Blessed Sacrament.[1] As a sign of veneration, the priest and deacon kiss the altar. When the occasion warrants, the priest may also incense the altar.[2]

The altar symbolizes the heart of the church. It is the Lord's table and the center of the eucharistic action. It has always been considered a symbol of Christ. That is why we cover the altar with a cloth, out of reverence for the celebration of the memorial of the Lord's sacrifice. We use candles at every liturgical service as a sign of veneration and festiveness. There also has to be a cross, clearly visible to the congregation, either on the altar or near it.[3]

To KISS the altar is to kiss Christ.

It is then understandable that we want to make ours this kiss of the celebrant. It evokes in our memory the many kisses of that sinful woman in the Pharisee's house. She could not cease to kiss Christ's feet, washing them with her tears. Great sins were forgiven her because she also loved greatly, the Gospel tells us (Lk 7:38). And we have so many faults to ask pardon for!

Now, by this kiss, the priest also signifies the union of the Spouse (Christ) with his Bride (the Church). And, indeed, what the priest is beginning to accomplish here is nothing other than to forge the union of the Church with her Master, of the soul with its Redeemer.

---

[1] GIRM, no. 84. If there is a tabernacle with the Blessed Sacrament in the sanctuary, a genuflection is made whenever anyone passes in front of the Blessed Sacrament.

[2] GIRM, no. 27.

[3] GIRM, no. 270.

Relics of saints inside the altar

During the first centuries, the altar-table was often a stone slab placed over the tomb of a martyr. Could the memorial of the death of the Savior be anywhere more fittingly celebrated than on the tombs of the faithful who had died for Christ? The saints, members of Christ, have been buried in Christ by charity. This is the origin of the custom of setting in the altar-stone a cavity (called the *sepulchre*) in which relics of martyrs are enclosed. St. John, in the Book of Revelation, says, "I saw beneath the altar the souls of all who had been slain for love of God's word" (6:90). Some people think that this statement refers to the habit of saying Mass over a martyr's tomb on certain occasions early in the life of the Church: It is as old as that.

Nowadays the Church sees it fitting to maintain the practice. However, the relics may be of any saint, even of nonmartyrs, and these may also be placed beneath the altar. Care is taken to have solid evidence of the authenticity of such relics.[4]

Incense is offered to God

St. John Chrysostom says that, "By its nature, the altar is a unique stone, for it is sanctified by the fact of the presence of Jesus Christ."[5] That is why at solemn Mass, the priest, after having kissed the altar, pays honor to it by incensing it.

Incense is a resinous substance which, when placed upon glowing charcoal, gives off a balsamic odor as it burns. It had a place in Israelite worship; in fact, the psalmist compares our prayers to the smoke of incense, rising up to heaven. In the Book of Revelation, it is seen as a symbol of the prayers of the saints.[6]

Incense was also used in pagan rites and for nonreligious purposes. It was used, for instance, to mask the stench which was not uncommon where crowds were gathered, honoring thus the consuls and magistrates. It was through this use that incense found its way into the liturgy.

---

4 See GIRM, no. 266.
5 St. John Chrysostom, *On 2 Corin.*, Hom. 20.3.
6 Rev 8:3–4; see also Ps 110:2

When paganism declined, the Church withdrew her earlier reservation about the use of incense. Gradually, toward the ninth century, she resorted in her liturgy to the use of this mark of honor as an expression of her veneration: of Christ himself; then of the bread and wine which were about to undergo transubstantiation, of the altar of sacrifice, of the cross, of the words of life contained in the Book of the Gospels, of the celebrant who acted in the person of Christ, and of all the faithful, the Mystical Body of Christ.

"We offer frankincense that rises up to the Lord: our desire to live a noble life which gives off the 'aroma of Christ.' To impregnate our words and actions with his aroma is to sow understanding and friendship." [7]

In the name of the Blessed Trinity

After the entrance song, and after having kissed the altar, the priest goes to the chair and with the whole assembly makes the sign of the cross, saying,

In the name of the Father, and of the Son, and of the Holy Spirit.

We all answer,

Amen.

We have been born through baptism to the life of grace under the sign of the cross and in the name of the Three Divine Persons; we have been strengthened in that life through the sacrament of Confirmation and under the same name of the Triune Godhead. It seems logical that we now approach the very source of spiritual life in the name of the most Blessed Trinity.

THROUGHOUT the Mass, we pay especial reverence to the name of Jesus.[8] St. Peter and St. John were arrested for proclaiming the resurrection of Jesus. When interrogated by the Sanhedrin, "By what

---

[7] J. Escrivá de Balaguer, *Christ Is Passing By* (New York: Scepter, 1974), no. 36; cf. 2 Cor 2:15.

[8] GIRM, nos. 233, 234. As a sign of reverence, a bow of the head is made by the priest when the Three Divine Persons are named together and at the name of Jesus, Mary, and the saint in whose honor Mass is celebrated.

power and by whose name have you men done this?" Peter answered, "By the name of Jesus Christ the Nazarene." And added, "For of all the names in the world given to men, this is the only one by which we can be saved" (Acts 4:12).

The priest's greeting to the entire Church

Through his greeting, the priest declares to us that the Lord is present. He accompanies his words with a gesture which may be seen as a delicately initiated embrace.

Sometimes the priest will greet us with a more elaborate formula, desiring that the grace of our Lord Jesus Christ, and the love of God, and the fellowship of the Holy Spirit be with us all. At other times, he will use a shorter greeting,

> *The Lord be with you.*

It reminds us of the angel's salutation to Mary (Lk 1:28), or St. Paul's to the Thessalonians (2 Thess 2:16), or even of Boaz's to the harvesters (Ruth 2:4).

This greeting and the congregation's response express the mystery of the gathered Church. It is the entire Church which is present, even though we may be just a few persons in the room. The Second Vatican Council tells us,

> In these Eucharistic communities, though frequently small and poor, or living in exile, Christ is present, and in virtue of his presence there is brought together the one, holy, catholic and apostolic Church.[9]

And Blessed Josemaría Escrivá writes,

> When I celebrate Mass with just one person to help me, the people are present also. I feel that there with me are all Catholics, all believers and also those who do not believe. All God's creatures are there—the earth and the sea and the sky, and the animals and plants—the whole of creation giving glory to the Lord.[10]

---

[9] LG, no. 26.
[10] J. Escrivá de Balaguer, *A Priest Forever*, Homily, p. 15.

In this greeting, the priest pours out all the love of his undivided heart, all the energies of a life devoted entirely to his brethren. "These ministers in the society of the faithful are able, by the sacred power of Orders, to offer sacrifice [the Holy Mass] and to forgive sins [sacrament of Penance], and they perform their priestly office publicly for men in the name of Christ." [11] It is then a wonderful opportunity to say our answer,

And also with you,

putting in it all our gratefulness.

We think of one moving reality: So many persons who have renounced clean and legitimate human love to place their lives at Christ's service and our service. It is time now to pay our debt to them, which we too often forget about.

Listen to this voice:

I ask all Christians to pray earnestly for us priests that we learn to perform the holy sacrifice in a holy way. I ask you to show a deep love for the Holy Mass. In this way you will encourage us priests to celebrate it respectfully, with divine and human dignity: to keep clean the vestments and other things used for worship, to act devoutly, to avoid rushing.[12]

We should include in our answer a vehement petition to our Lord for the sanctity of priests. Because as St. John Chrysostom points out,

When the priests are holy, the entire Church is resplendent with virtues; when they are not holy, faith weakens. When you see a tree with withered leaves, you judge that there should be some vice in the roots; likewise when you see an unruly people you should understand that their priests are not holy.[13]

---

[11] Second Vatican Council, decree *Presbyterorum Ordinis* [= PO], no. 2; cf. Council of Trent, session 27, ch. 1, c. 1 (Denz. 1764, 1771).

[12] J. Escrivá de Balaguer, *Christ Is Passing By*, p. 15.

[13] St. John Chrysostom, *Catena Aurea*.

7. Penitential Rite

My sacrifice is this broken spirit, you will not scorn this crushed and broken heart (Ps 51:17).

We have just announced with the entrance song that Christ is with us, and we are ready to unite ourselves to him, who is the Good Shepherd and King of Eternal Glory. These titles make us understand: first, the spirit of confidence with which we have to approach him and, second, the sacred respect and reverence which pervades the heavenly liturgy.

Who would not revere and praise your name, O Lord? You alone are holy, and all the pagans will come and adore you for the many acts of justice you have shown (Rev 15:4).

We feel now more than ever the need for purification, for penance. We welcome the *invitation* of the priest:

To prepare ourselves to celebrate the sacred mysteries,
let us call to mind our sins.
Let us acknowledge our failures and ask the Lord for pardon and
*   strength . . .*
for he is full of gentleness and compassion.

And then *silence* . . . We seem to hear the words of Isaiah: "Come now, let us set things right, says the Lord: Though your sins be like scarlet, they may become white as snow; though they be crimson red, they may become white as wool" (Is 1:18).

THE penitential rite before the Eucharist is of the greatest antiquity. One of the oldest pieces of evidence about liturgical matters which we possess, the *Didaché* (or *Teaching of the Apostles*), shows us that this penitential rite was already the practice among Christians at the beginning of the second century: "On the Lord's day, we meet together; break the bread and give thanks, after having first confessed our sins so that our sacrifice may be pure." These words echo what St. Paul wrote one century earlier: "Let every man examine himself, before he eat of this bread."

The penitential rite makes us aware of our unworthiness. It is not an abstract reminder of guilt, but the actual realization and admission of our sins and weaknesses. We ask pardon for our sins as we say,

I confess to almighty God,
and to you, my brothers and sisters . . .

We grovel and accuse ourselves of our sins in the sight of heaven.

Now you realize how much you have made Jesus suffer, and you are filled with sorrow. How easy it is to ask his pardon and weep for your past betrayals! Such is your longing for atonement that you cannot contain it in your breast!

Fine. But don't forget that the spirit of penance consists mainly in the fulfillment of the duty of each moment, however costly it may be.[1]

We have sinned not only before heaven, but also in the sight of the earth. Every sin you or I commit lets down the whole Christian community, doesn't it? Just as you apologize to your partner when you have made a perfectly rotten stroke at tennis, so when you have sinned you want to apologize to your fellow Christians; for you have let them all down.

There is a too-common tendency to want to deny or to excuse our wrong-doing and to put the blame for it on someone else: We accuse others in order to excuse ourselves, we reproach others for having incited us to do wrong. We resort to these wretched subterfuges, which deceive no one, merely to lead ourselves astray with them.

Let us take a good honest look at our own lives. How is it that sometimes we just can't find those few minutes it would take to finish lovingly the work we have to do, which is the very means of our sanctification? Why do we neglect

---

[1] J. Escrivá de Balaguer, *The Way of the Cross* (New York: Scepter, 1983), p. 81.

our family duties? Why that tendency to rush through our prayers, or through the holy sacrifice of the Mass? How are we so lacking in calm and serenity when it comes to fulfilling the duties of our state, and yet so unhurried as we indulge in our own whims? You might say these are trifling matters. You are right, they are, but these trifles are the oil, the fuel we need to keep our flame alive and our light shining.[2]

Now THAT we are before God, let us begin by being sincere:

I have sinned through my own fault . . .
in my thoughts and in my words,
in what I have done,
and in what I have failed to do.

This act of deep repentance, a *mea culpa*, when the hand strikes the breast, is an old biblical gesture. It brings consolation to the sinner in his racking sorrow; for is it not written that the humble man's prayer pierces the clouds and that he shall be heard before the Most High? [3]

The Church in heaven and the Church on earth are witnesses to our sin, and we beg their brotherly help in interceding for our pardon. First, the Blessed Virgin Mary, who never sinned; because "to Jesus we always go, and to him we always return, through Mary." [4] Then, we ask all the angels, who fought against the pride of the rebellious ones; all the saints, who were also sinners; all Christians on earth to pray for us so that we be truly sorry for our sins.

THE MISSAL carries three forms of the penitential rite. At the end of each, the priest takes refuge with his brethren in the mercy of God:

May almighty God have mercy on us,
forgive us our sins,
and bring us to everlasting life.

---

[2] J. Escrivá de Balaguer, *Friends of God*, no. 41.
[3] Sir 35:16–17.
[4] J. Escrivá de Balaguer, *The Way*, no. 495.

The penitential rite of the Mass is not a sacramental confession; therefore, it does not bring immediate remission of mortal sins. Forgiveness of mortal sins has to be obtained in the sacrament of Penance. It is also important to remember that a person who has committed a mortal sin cannot go to Communion unless he goes to confession beforehand. But the penitential rite, if it is said with true contrition, helps to obtain pardon for present venial sins, as well as to stir up new sorrow for past sins that have already been forgiven. In this way, it helps us to purify ourselves and so to take better part in the Holy Mass.[5]

"Amen," we answer. Our soul overcomes the shame of contemplating our impurities before God's splendor.

For Sunday Masses, it is possible to have the blessing and sprinkling with holy water in place of the penitential rite. The *Kyrie* is also omitted. This is a visible reminder of our baptism and of the need for purification from the stains of sins we committed after baptism.

SORROW for our sins—the greatest saints never ceased to foster and advocate this most holy interior disposition. In their souls, it was something much greater than a series of isolated acts of passing impulses. The expressions of deep sorrow which they often uttered were nothing more than outward signs of a permanent and stable inward attitude eager to find an outlet.

> Indeed, God's generosity toward these great souls makes them acknowledge all the more sorrowfully the enormity of their ingratitude toward him. In the splendor of the divine light, the slightest shadow seems monstrous darkness, the slightest fault seems an enormous crime. . . . So, we should always live in a state of repentance, until the last moment of our life, and not let even one day pass without trying to blot out our faults with tears of sorrow. Is it not true that we forget our miseries very quickly, with a levity at times quite frightening?

[5] See Sacred Congregation for the Doctrine of the Faith, *Pastoral Norms concerning the Administration of the General Sacramental Absolution* (July 1972), no. 1. See also C. Burke, *The Mass Explained* (Manila: Sinag-Tala, 1986), p. 5.

I do not ask you, far from it, to think of them all the time, so that they become an obsession with you, sapping all your healthy energies. No, but lament them every day in your prayer, in a general way, without trying to remember particular instances: for this would only weaken your true repentance. Then, lift up your eyes to the Lord of mercy.

Would it not be a very good thing to ask pardon for your faults precisely during those moments when the penitential rite is being said, genuinely convinced that you too contributed to the passion of your Lord; and to humiliate yourself, like the priest and with the priest, every time he humiliates himself during the Mass? [6]

---

[6] Bernard Vasconcelos, *Your Mass* (New York: Scepter, 1960), pp. 22–23.

8. *The* Kyrie

Son of David, Jesus, have mercy on me! (Mk 10:46).

After having bridged the gap between God's love and our feeble love through penance, we again feel the need to express our joy. The presence of Christ makes us break into praise with the *Kyrie* and the *Gloria*, and into petition with the Opening Prayer or Collect.

To give glory to God and to beg his mercy are two reasons why man turns to God: It is because we know that God is almighty that we ask him to have mercy on us. All the nuances of these two inseparable purposes are expressed in the *Kyrie*.

Kyrie eleison means "Lord, have mercy." This formula comes straight from the Gospel. Both the blind man of Jericho and the Canaanite woman cried, "Son of David, have mercy on me!" [1] And the lepers cried aloud, "Jesus, Master, have pity on us!" (Lk 17:13).

Blessed Josemaría Escrivá invites us to consider:

> Don't you too feel the same urge to cry out? You who also are waiting at the side of the way, of this highway of life that is so very short? You who need more light, you who need more grace to make up your mind to seek holiness? Don't you feel an urgent need to cry out, "Jesus, son of David, have pity on me"? What a beautiful aspiration for you to repeat again and again! [2]

This cry of supplication passed into the liturgy of Christians, for we too have to call upon the divine mercy. But it is obvious that this prayer presupposes a previous declaration of our guilt: It is the completion of an earlier invocation. It is, in reality, the response to a litany. The *Kyrie* is a remnant of those litanic dialogues, of those frequently long prayers which accompanied the procession of the

---

[1] See Mk 10:46–52; Mt 15:21ff.
[2] J. Escrivá de Balaguer, *Friends of God*, no. 195.

celebrant up to the altar. It originated in the Greek-speaking East, where the Spanish pilgrim Eteria heard it sung in Jerusalem about the year 390. You probably know that Greek, rather than Latin, was the prevalent liturgical language of the early Church. From the East, the litany passed into the Latin Church.

Toward the eighth century, the pope reduced the acclamations to just nine. The first three were addressed to God the Father. The second group of acclamations, which in Rome became *Christe eleison* ("Christ, have mercy on us"), were addressed to God the Son; and the last three invocations to the Holy Spirit.

It seems that acclamations like these were also used as praises and hymns with which the people received a triumphant warrior after a battle. They celebrated his victory, as well as sought his favor. And that is precisely the meaning the acclamations keep, transposed to the supernatural level. The *Kyrie* is a song by which the faithful praise the Lord and implore his mercy.[3]

As in any acclamation coming from a humble servant, in the *Kyrie* we sincerely pay homage to our Lord and present to him our supplication. We have nothing, but we hope to receive everything from him—especially his mercy, which is indispensable for us to be justified.

The *Kyrie* is also a clear and vibrant profession of faith, because when we acclaim Christ as our Lord, we express our determined resolution not to serve two lords, but him alone.

Nowadays the *Kyrie* is prayed by all—that is, alternately by the congregation and the choir or cantor. As a rule, each of the acclamations is said twice; but in some circumstances, it may be said more than twice, or a short verse (called a *trope*) may be interposed. If the *Kyrie* is not sung, it is to be recited, either in English or in the original Greek.

3 GIRM, no. 30.

9. *The* Gloria

Glory to God in the highest heaven, and peace to his people on earth (Lk 2:14).

The *Gloria* or "Greater Doxology" is of great antiquity. Its style supports the theory that it is among the earliest of all Christian hymns. There is no phrase in it which does not also appear either in the epistles of St. Paul or in the writings of St. John.

The first Christians used to sing it in their meetings, usually early in the morning. They saw in the rising sun a symbol of Christ, a great light which comes to dispel darkness. Soon it was introduced in the Mass, but only on Christmas day. In the sixth century, Pope St. Symmachus extended its use to the main solemnities, Sundays, and feasts of martyrs, but only for the Mass celebrated by the bishop. Toward the tenth century, it began to be used more or less as it is now.

THE *Gloria* is sung or said on Sundays outside Advent or Lent, on solemnities and feasts, and in special, more solemn celebrations. It is usually sung by the congregation, or by the congregation alternately with the choir, or by the choir alone. If not sung, it is to be recited either by all together or in alternation.

With the *Gloria*, the Church, assembled in the Holy Spirit, praises and entreats the Father and the Lamb.[1] It begins with the words the angels said to the shepherds on Christmas night (Lk 2:14), for which reason this composition is also known as the Angelic Hymn:

Glory to God in the highest
and peace to his people on earth.

The shepherds, being simple men, were overwhelmed with enthusiasm and excitement. They felt they had to sing of such a sublime

---

[1] GIRM, no. 31.

mystery. And then, enlightened by the Light of the world, doubtless they realized that they should glorify that great mystery not only through the music of their rustic flutes, but also in their hearts.

We must be like them: a living testimony to God's glory.

Of what use would be all our acts of piety, if we did not amend our life, if we did not fulfill our professional duties?

We do not want to proclaim the glories of God while our mind and will are clothed in vanity.

We do not want to speak of them, while our heart is full of bitterness toward our neighbor. You and I must not act thus.

AFTER the angels' shout of joy, we can distinguish two parts in the *Gloria*. The first is addressed to the Father:

> *Lord God, heavenly King,*
> *almighty God, and Father,*
> *We worship you, we give you thanks,*
> *we praise you for your glory.*

Man must worship the Creator before asking favors of him. There can be no peace on earth unless we recognize the sovereignty of God.

With all the strength of our souls, we affirm our abiding in God when we confess his glory. But notice that in the course of the Mass, we have many opportunities to thank God for his favors to us. Here we thank him, not for what he has done, but for what he is: *propter magnam gloriam tuam*, for his great glory, for his immensity, for his incomprehensibility.

The second part is addressed to Jesus Christ:

> *Lord Jesus Christ, only Son of the Father,*
> *Lord God, Lamb of God,*
> *you take away the sin of the world:*
> *have mercy on us;*
> *you are seated at the right hand of the Father:*
> *receive our prayer.*

The soul praises and blesses the Son of God, the "only Son of the Father." He himself, the Good Shepherd, became the sacrificial Lamb in order to save all men by his death—on a cross.

And this spotless Lamb did not hesitate to become the "man of sorrows" and to burden himself with our sins, in order to take away the sins of the world, in order to reconcile man with God.

He had such compassion on our infirmities that he left behind his seat in heaven "at the right hand of the Father."

Greater love than this no man has, that a man lay down his life for his friends. Now, if he is such a friend of ours, why should we not ask him humbly to have mercy on us?

He will listen to our pleas, because he said "ask and you shall receive." Therefore, let us ask him humbly, confidently, and with perseverance: "Receive our prayer." We poor men can never stop begging from God. May we never lack the faith and humility to continue doing so.

We can find in this hymn the four reasons for which the Mass is said. These should also be our dispositions when we participate in the Mass:

> *Praise of God:* "We worship you . . . , we praise you . . . "
> *Thanksgiving:* "We give you thanks . . . for your glory."
> *Atonement and sorrow for sins:* "You take away the sin of the world: have mercy on us."
> *Petition:* "Receive our prayer."

Here our souls surge with these sentiments which will mount as the Mass goes on. Thus the soul sings the *Gloria*, even though the lips may only be reciting it. The soul sings in the name of the entire creation, yearning for the coming of the kingdom of God, which is announced and effected in the Mass.

This most beautiful of hymns is brought to its end in sublime simplicity:

> *For you alone are the Holy One,*
> *you alone are the Lord,*
> *you alone are the Most High,*
> *Jesus Christ,*
> *with the Holy Spirit,*
> *in the glory of God the Father. Amen.*

This act of faith in Christ and in the Blessed Trinity has its origin in the Greek liturgy of the first centuries. When the priest showed the body of Christ before Communion, the people acclaimed the Lord by saying, "You alone are the Holy One, you are the Lord, Jesus Christ, in the glory of the Father." Then the words, "you alone are the Most High" were added, taken from Psalm 82, verse 19, which have always been applied to Christ.

10. *Opening Prayer or Collect*

"Anything you ask for from the Father he will grant in my name.
Ask and you will receive" (Jn 16:23–24).

According to the ancient plan of the Roman Mass, the Collect is the
first prayer which is proper of the priest. Thus, it is one of the presidential prayers (the others are the Prayer over the Gifts and the
Prayer after Communion). The introductory rites reach their apex in
the Opening Prayer. It is not enough to have adored and praised
God, and to have asked for mercy. We also need a concise formula
that summarizes the petitions or intentions of the celebration.

The Opening Prayer is also called the Collect because it sums up
and gathers together all the intentions of the day's sacrifice. Histori-
cally, this title recalls the old custom of Rome, where, about the
fourth century, it was the practice for the whole community to
gather in one church so that they might proceed with solemnity to
the temple chosen for the celebration of the day's Mass. In this second sense, the Collect is the prayer of the *plebs collecta*, the prayer of
the assembled people.

"Let us pray," the celebrant intones, asking the people to join him,
for this is a public and collective prayer. In olden times, after this
invitation, the people were invited to kneel down (with the *flectamus
genua*) and devote a few moments to private prayer. This ancient custom still survives in the rites of Holy Week (Good Friday). Nowadays we stand and observe a brief *silence* to help us realize that we are
in God's presence and to call our petitions to mind.

The priest then says the Opening Prayer in the attitude called
orans. This gesture is an entirely natural one in prayer and was in use
among the Jews. Pagans prayed with their hands held above their
heads, palms turned upward, in the attitude of one who expects to
receive a gift. As can be seen in the wall paintings of the catacombs,
the Church had no objection to this universal gesture. Christians,
however, changed the position of the hands, making the palms face
each other "so as to resemble those of the Lord on the cross," and at

the same time lowering the arms, so as "not to raise up our hands ostentatiously," as Tertullian says.

In general, we ask that we may be made worthy of the promises of Christ our Lord; that God may "free us from sin and bring us the joy that lasts for ever";[1] that he may "give us freedom of spirit and health in mind and body to do your work on earth." [2]

We may also ask for our personal needs, material and spiritual. However, at this moment, we should go beyond our personal concerns and ask for as many crowns as those who enter the combat of Christian life. Our prayer to God the Father will then be not merely an individual petition but an expression and fulfillment of the unity of the faithful gathered through Christ in the Holy Spirit. "Watch over your chosen family. Give undying life to all who have been born again in baptism." [3] "Father of light, from whom every good gift comes, send your Spirit into our lives . . . , open the horizons of our minds. Loosen our tongues to sing your praise in words beyond the power of speech. . . ." [4]

Structure of the Opening Prayer

The Opening Prayer always begins with an *invocation* to God. It is followed either by a statement of the *grounds* on which we base our confidence that our prayer will be granted, or by a reference (*evocation*) to the mystery or feast being celebrated. Then the *petition* follows, which expounds to a greater or lesser degree upon the subject of the request being made. Then comes the *conclusion*, which is invariably based upon a request for the intercession of our sole Mediator, Jesus Christ our Lord, and upon homage to the indivisible Trinity.

Here is an example showing us the elements and structure of the Opening Prayer:

Invocation: *Almighty God,*

Grounds: *our hope and our strength, without you we falter.*

[1] Roman Missal, Opening Prayer, 14th week in Ordinary Time.
[2] Roman Missal, Opening Prayer, 32nd week in Ordinary Time.
[3] Roman Missal, Opening Prayer, Easter Sunday.
[4] Roman Missal, Opening Prayer, Pentecost.

Petition: *Help us to follow Christ and to live according to
               your will.*

Conclusion: *We ask this through our Lord Jesus Christ, your
               Son, who lives and reigns with you and the Holy
               Spirit, one God, for ever and ever.*[5]

Or take this other example, this time of an Opening Prayer inspired
by the mystery being commemorated:

Invocation: *Lord, our God,*

Evocation: *with the birth of your Son, your glory breaks on the
               world. Through the night hours of the darkened
               earth we your people watch for the coming of your
               promised Son.*

Petition: *As we wait, give us a foretaste of the joy that you
               will grant us when the fullness of his glory has filled
               the earth,*

Conclusion: *who lives and reigns with you for ever and ever.*[6]

On the feasts of our Blessed Mother, the angels, and the saints, it is
customary to invoke their intercession in the Collect.[7] There is often
a reference to some title which is proper to them or to some virtue
they lived in an exemplary way. Thus we ask the intercession of the
Blessed Virgin in the beautiful Opening Prayer of the solemnity of
the Immaculate Conception:

*Father, you prepared the Virgin to be the worthy Mother of your Son.
You let her share beforehand in the salvation Christ would bring by his
death, and kept her sinless from the first moment of her conception. Help*

---

[5] Roman Missal, Opening Prayer, 11th week in Ordinary Time.

[6] Roman Missal, Opening Prayer, December 25, Mass at Midnight.

[7] We find in the Bible many instances of the special mediation of the Virgin Mary, subordinate to Christ's: Jn 2:3–5ff. We also find many examples of the intercession of angels and holy men on behalf of others: in the Old Testament, Ex 15:14ff.; Jb 5:1, 33:23, 42:8; Ps 99:6; Jer 15:1, 18:20, 42:2; Ez 9:8; Dn 9:15–19; Am 7:2, etc.; and in the New Testament, Jn 4:47; Mt 15:22; Mk 8:22, 9:16; Lk 4:38; Jas 5:16; Rom 15:30; 1 Thes 1:2; Acts 12:5; Phil 1:3; Col 1:9.

us by her prayers to live in your presence without sin. We ask this through our Lord Jesus Christ, your Son, who lives and reigns with you and the Holy Spirit, one God, for ever and ever.

In spite of the variety of formulas, we always ask for the same thing: what is essential in our Christian life. Besides, there are not too many words in the vocabulary of persons in love. The result is that we may unconsciously sink into routine and shallowness, because of the brevity of the Collect. So that this does not happen, we must exert the effort needed to grasp the different nuances of each prayer and their supernatural dimension. We may be asking always for the same thing, but we should do it as if we are making each petition for the first time.

The Lord is true to his word: Whatever we ask of him will be granted, if it is good for our sanctity. He promised to hear our prayer. But when he told us, "Ask and it shall be given to you," was he referring to what is essential or to unimportant things? Unwittingly, we may be basing our love for God on earthly benefits and forgetting about our personal sanctity.

It is now time to unite our minds and hearts with the supplication which the priest directs to God on behalf of all. We should do so with faith, without hesitation, as St. James recommends to us: "One must ask in faith, one must not hesitate; one who hesitates is like a wave out at sea, driven to and fro by the wind; such a man must not hope to win any gift from the Lord" (Jas 1:6–8).

The *Amen*

The Opening Prayer ends with the word *Amen*. We make the prayer our own and give our assent by this acclamation. Its translation could be: "So be it!" or "Be it done so!" The Jews used it to agree on a contract and also to express a wish.

Amen is the last word of the New Testament: It closes the Revelation. *Amen* is truly the last word in all prayer. It is the last word, too, in holiness, which is man's perfect adherence to the will of God. It is to say, "As you wish." "My Lord and my God: into your hands I abandon the past and the present and the future, what is small and what is great, what amounts to a little and what amounts to a lot, things temporal and things eternal." [8] I say *Amen* to all that you ask of me.

With that *Amen*, therefore, we acknowledge sincerely our total dependence on God. It is only fitting that we exert the effort to pronounce it decisively. In doing so, we will be happy to hear through the veil of our faith what the Lord told Moses: "This request, too, which you have just made, I will carry out, because you have found favor with me and you are my intimate friend" (Ex 33:17).

"We have this confidence in God: that he hears us whenever we ask for anything according to his will" (1 Jn 5:14).

---

[8] J. Escrivá de Balaguer, *The Way of the Cross*, p. 68.

PART III
LITURGY OF THE WORD

A. God Is Talking to Us

Only God knew with how much impatience the disciples gathered in the Upper Room were waiting for the arrival of the Lord. They did not know why and what, but they were sure something very important was going to happen. The Master had told them to prepare everything for the celebration of the Passover.

When Jesus arrived, they received him as usual, perhaps with a mixture of that sweet and gentle fear that the presence of the supernatural produces in the human soul. Surely, they must have been grateful to God for having given them the chance of sitting at the table once more with the person for whom mankind had been yearning for centuries. And he precisely addressed himself to them before anyone else. They could not explain why he had chosen them; there was no human explanation for it. But they constantly gave thanks to God for the election. Their countenances showed their intimate joy.

Had they known their unworthiness, they would have fled in shame. But they also knew that Jesus came to heal the sick and the weak. So, there they remained, perhaps feeling more in need than anybody else. After all it was the Master who sought them and chose them. He knew pretty well what he was doing. Their role was simply to allow themselves to be loved and to exert every effort to correspond to that love.

11. *At the Table of the Bread and the Word*

*"I am the bread of life. He who comes to me will never be hungry;
he who believes in me will never thirst"* (Jn 6:35).

As soon as Jesus arrived in the Upper Room, all sat down and
focused on him all their power of concentration. Then, the Master
began to speak at length, as he had spoken on other occasions: at the
foot of the mountain, in the synagogue, from a boat in the middle of
the lake, perhaps in someone's house. . . . But this time, there was
such an atmosphere of intimacy . . .

In the Mass, after having welcomed him with joy and purified our
love through our contrition, we are ready to listen to Jesus. Like the
apostles before the Last Supper, we too are going to sit down. The
Master is going to talk to us—by means of the sacred readings of the
Mass. By faith we know that when the Scriptures are read in the
Church, God himself is speaking to his people, and Christ, present
in his own word, is proclaiming the Gospel.[1]

Besides his eucharistic presence, "in another very genuine way,
Christ is also present in the Church as she preaches. For the Gospel
which she proclaims is the word of God, and it is only in the name of
Christ, the Incarnate Word of God, and only by his authority and
with his help that it is preached, so that there might be 'one flock
resting secure in one shepherd.' "[2]

In the teachings of Christ, and particularly in his crucifixion,
divine revelation reaches its peak.[3] The liturgy of the word serves,
then, as a preparation for the eucharistic liturgy: "When therefore
the faithful hear the word of God, they should realize that the won-
ders it proclaims culminate in the paschal mystery, whose memorial
is celebrated sacramentally in the Mass."[4]

---

[1] GIRM, no. 9.
[2] MF, no. 37.
[3] See Heb 1:1–2.
[4] Sacred Congregation of Rites, Instruction on Eucharistic Worship, *Eucharisticum
Mysterium* (May 25, 1967), no. 10.

The mystery of salvation is announced in the Mass with the proclamation of the word. Afterward, during the eucharistic liturgy, what
has been announced becomes reality. This way the bond between
the word and the eucharistic action (which culminates with the
Consecration) becomes evident. Word and action, therefore, are
united. The word announces and explains the action, and the latter
brings to fulfillment what has been announced with the word. For,
in "the celebration of the Mass . . . it is the purpose of the liturgy
of the word to develop the close connection between the preaching
and hearing of the word of God and the eucharistic mystery." [5] The
sacraments are sacraments of faith, and faith has its origin and sustenance in the word.

This link between the liturgy of the word and the sacrifice can
help us understand how we should participate in this preliminary
part of the eucharistic celebration as a manifestation of the common
priesthood we possess as faithful. Only if we receive the message
with fitting dispositions during the readings shall we be present at
the Eucharistic Prayer with the necessary faith and love to offer ourselves with Christ and to be intimately united to him during
Communion.

In ancient times, the catechumens were allowed to attend only the
first part of the Mass. They were not permitted to participate in the
true core of Christian worship, because they had not yet been baptized and therefore did not possess the royal priesthood. As catechumens, they were allowed to be present only during the catechetical
part—that is, during the readings and explanations of the word of
God.

What a pity if during the first part of the Mass we were just waiting for the offering of the gifts—as if the Offertory were the real
beginning of the Mass. We cannot keep the attitude of being satisfied
as long as we arrive not later than "after the Creed," as often happened in earlier times.

The liturgy of the word is especially necessary in our days. However, the importance we give to the word of God should not obscure
the value of the eucharistic liturgy. Neither should we fall into the
opposite error, because the Church has always venerated the sacred

---

[5] *Eucharisticum Mysterium*, no. 10; see also PO, no. 4.

Scriptures just as she venerates the body of the Lord. Especially in her liturgy, the Church unceasingly receives and offers to the faithful the Bread of life from the table of God's word and of Christ's body.[6]

The first Christians understood this reality very well. Apart from the celebration of the Eucharist, they gathered together to listen with veneration to the sacred Scriptures. Nowadays the Church continues to recommend the liturgical celebrations of the word. For "the force and power in the word of God is so great that it stands as the support and energy of the Church, the strength of faith for her sons, the food of the soul, the pure and everlasting source of spiritual life." Through this word, "the voice of the Holy Spirit sounds again and again in the words of the prophets and apostles." [7]

Sacred Scriptures, the way to know God

As the Constitution on Divine Revelation of the Second Vatican Council teaches us, God wanted to reveal himself and to make known the mystery of his will (see Eph 1:9). His will was that men should have access to the Father, through Christ, the Word made flesh, in the Holy Spirit, and thus become sharers in the divine nature. By this revelation, then, the invisible God, from the fullness of his love, addresses men as his friend, and stays among them to invite and receive them into his own company.[8] This is how, without looking for it or deserving it, we came to know the intimate truth, both about God and about our own salvation.

This truth is made known to us through the sacred Scriptures, which, together with the sacred Tradition, "are like a mirror, in which the Church, during her pilgrim journey here on earth, contemplates God, from whom she receives everything, until such time as she is brought to see him face to face as he really is." [9]

What we hear during the liturgy of the word is truth about God and the narrative of the marvels God performed among men. Its culmination is the paschal mystery of the death and resurrection of Christ, which is perpetuated in the Eucharist.

---

[6] See Second Vatican Council, Dogmatic Constitution *Dei Verbum* [= DV], no. 21.

[7] DV, no. 21.

[8] DV, no. 2.

[9] DV, no. 7.

Therefore, the central theme of the readings is always Christ. As an innocent lamb, he merited life for us by his blood, which he freely shed. In him, God reconciled us with himself and with one another, freeing us from the bondage of the devil and sin. By suffering for us, he not only gave us an example that we could follow, but also opened up a way. If we follow this path, life and death are made holy and take on a new meaning.[10]

All the readings, both of the Old and the New Testaments, are oriented toward Christ. In his wisdom, God has so brought it about that the New Testament should be hidden in the Old Testament, and that the Old Testament should be made manifest in the New. Hence, the New Testament sheds light on and explains what was earlier announced and signified with different figures in the Old Testament.[11]

We will get to know Christ better by listening to the reading of the holy Scriptures with pious attention. Our lives are linked to his life because we must transform ourselves into him to be pleasing to God the Father. By carefully listening to the word of God and reflecting on it, we will realize who and how Christ was, what he said and did, what he expects of us, and how we are to go about accomplishing the task he entrusted to us. Gradually, we will enter into the intimacy of God and discover the meaning of our own existence. And, as a consequence, we will get to know how to do—always and in everything—the will of God.

Actual, life-giving word

But that is not all. We cannot be satisfied with having at our disposal a divine means to know what God's love did for men in the past.

Certainly, that is not a little gift at all. But reality goes beyond that. The word of God, proclaimed by the Church, does not only tell us of what happened in times past. No, it is not something lost in history. It is something which is being accomplished and fulfilled today, here and now, because God continues his work of salvation through the ministry of his Mystical Body. In the word of God the divine covenant is announced; in the Eucharist the new and everlasting

---

[10] Second Vatican Council, Dogmatic Constitution *Gaudium et Spes* [= GS], no. 22.
[11] DV, nos. 15–16.

covenant is renewed. We know very well that in any Mass being said right now, the sacrifice of Calvary, with all its sanctifying power, is being renewed. And this renewal of the paschal event brings with it the actualization of the history of salvation in a mysterious but living and efficacious manner. This is why the Mass sums up the entire history of salvation as its source and apex.

With the eyes of our faith, we may now contemplate Jesus of Nazareth in the synagogue proclaiming, "This scripture which I have read in your hearing is today fulfilled" (Lk 4:21).

Actually, it is as it sounds. Here and now, in this temple where we are gathered, the announcements of the prophets and the events narrated by the evangelists are accomplished. Here, too, God the Father comes to meet his children through Christ. In this Mass, God asks us: Do you love me? Do you want to be my disciple? Do you want to have a part with me in eternal life? Are you ready to accompany me in the holocaust of the cross?

If we are to grow in the knowledge of the written word of God, we must prepare ourselves by prayer so that we may receive the light which the Holy Spirit is always ready to grant us. The way to a more effective understanding of holy Scripture—by reading, meditating, and studying—lies in a more intense life of prayer and a greater intimacy in dealing with God. A profound understanding of the word of God cannot be found in philology, archaeology, sociology, psychology, or any other human science; it can only be found with the light that God gives us when there is holiness of life. We need the humility that comes from dealing with God in our prayer to be able to walk in the brilliant light of faith without being blinded. Only piety can confer a certain connaturality and put us at ease with divine things; no rational schemes can do that for us.[12]

This word, being actual, living, and efficacious, has the power to transform, modify, and change the face of heaven and earth. It does not only announce and communicate a message, but also produces always the effect wanted by God.

"It is not a matter of just thinking about Jesus, of recalling some scenes of his life. We must be completely involved and play a part in

---

[12] See Leo XIII, *Providentissimus Deus*, November 18, 1893; Pius XII, *Divino Afflante Spiritu*, September 30, 1943.

his life. We should follow him as closely as Mary his Mother did, as closely as the first Twelve, the holy women, the crowds that pressed about him. If we do this without holding back, Christ's words will enter deep into our soul and will really change us." [13]

Today, as always, the word of God continues to exert its influence on the evolution of history. It can change the direction of the entire world. It can change our life. And it is precisely the force of this word which turns the bread and wine into the body and blood of Christ, thus making the paschal event present and renewing the work of our redemption.

The right interpretation

The word of God has to be accepted joyfully as it is proposed for belief by the teaching authority of the Church. The message of God contained in the Scriptures will be clear and unmistakable to each one of us, if we allow ourselves to be guided and illumined by the Magisterium of the Church. Pope Paul VI emphasized to the theologians:

> It is logical, then, for us to follow the Magisterium of the Church as a guiding star in carrying on our investigations into these mysteries, for the divine Redeemer has entrusted the safeguarding and the explanation of the written or transmitted word of God to her. And we are convinced that "whatever has been preached and believed throughout the whole Church with true catholic faith since the days of antiquity is true, even if it not be subject to rational investigation, and even if it not be explained in words." [14]

We cannot ignore or push aside the guidance of the Church if we want to know what God is telling us. The theologian, the exegete, the ordinary Christian must render "obedience to faith" (Rom 16:26), within the one true Church established by Jesus Christ, if they are to understand rightly the word of God. They must accept

---

[13] J. Escrivá de Balaguer, *Christ Is Passing By*, no. 107.
[14] MF, no. 22; quotation from St. Augustine, *Against Julian*, VI, 5.11 (PL 44:829).

on faith the canonical and historical character of Scripture, as well as its immunity from error, its authenticity, and its inspired character, precisely as the Church so teaches. They must approach the Bible with faith in God, who is its principal author and who guarantees its freedom from error. This faith is possible only within the Church, and furthermore it is incompatible with error.

We need a great faith to recognize that we possess the truth. God cannot allow that the things his Church has been teaching for twenty centuries with the assistance of the Holy Spirit should be permeated with error. So many martyrs have given their lives for these truths. So many of our ancestors have found the reason of their existence in upholding the true faith and transmitting it to us.

The word of God is also judgment

We should not forget that when we have heard the word of God, we can no longer be the same persons we were before. Either we allow ourselves to be captivated and transformed by it, or we resist its action, thus despising the hand of God. This is what we mean by saying that the word of God is also judgment. It serves as a condemnation if we do not accept the salvation it offers; for the Lord said,

> "Had I not performed such works among them as no one has ever done before, and spoken to them, they would not be guilty of sin; but now they do not have excuse for their sin" (Jn 15:24).

In considering these facts, it is fitting that we dispose ourselves to listen to the word of God with the simplicity with which our Blessed Mother listened to Jesus in Nazareth; with the admiration of the doctors of the Law in the Temple; with the joyful hope of the paralytics who were cured upon listening to the words of Jesus; with the generous disposition of Zacchaeus, firmly resolved to put into practice the teaching he had just received, even though it might change the course of his life and expose him to shame.

It is now time to be attentive to the proclamation of the word, with full piety, telling our Lord with a sincere heart: "Speak, Lord, for your servant is listening" (2 Sam 3:10).

PART III
LITURGY OF THE WORD (*Continued*)

B. From the First Reading to the Prayer of the Faithful
Readings from Scripture and the chants between the readings form the main part of the liturgy of the word. These elements are arranged in the following order:

> First Reading
> Responsorial Psalm
> Second Reading (only on Sundays and greater celebrations)
> Gospel Acclamation (*Alleluia* or another chant)
> Gospel

And after these come the:

> Homily
> Profession of Faith (Creed)
> General Intercessions (Prayer of the Faithful)

These elements develop the liturgy of the word, and with them the first part of the Mass concludes.

In the readings from the Scripture, God speaks to his people, opening up to them the mystery of redemption and salvation, and nourishing their spirit. Christ is present to the faithful through his own word. These readings are explained and expanded with the homily. Through the chants, the people make God's word their own; through the Profession of Faith, they affirm their adherence to it. Finally, having been nourished by this word, they make their petitions in the general intercessions for the needs of the Church and for the salvation of the whole world.[1]

---

[1] GIRM, no. 31.

12. Scriptural Readings

The word of God is something alive and active: it cuts like any double-edged sword but more finely: it can slip through the place where the soul is divided from the spirit, or joints from the marrow; it can judge the secret emotions and thoughts (Heb 4:12).

Distribution of readings

On Sundays and holy days, we usually find three readings, arranged thus: the first from the Old Testament, the second from the writings of an apostle, and the third from a Gospel. Thus, God's own teaching brings the Christian people to a knowledge of the continuity of the work of salvation.[1]

The present order of readings for the Mass is an arrangement of the biblical passages. It provides the faithful with a knowledge of the whole of God's word.[2] By following a plan of readings through the year, the treasures of the Bible are made fully accessible to the faithful. That "warm and living love for the Scripture"[3] which the Church bids us to have is thereby fostered. The advantage of having a single order of readings for the whole Church is obvious. All the faithful will everywhere be able to hear the same readings on any given day.[4]

The more important biblical passages are featured on Sundays and solemnities of the Lord. In this way, the more significant parts of God's revealed word are read to the assembly of the faithful within a reasonable period of time. Weekdays present a second series of texts from Scripture, and in a sense these complement the message of salvation explained on Sundays and solemnities of the Lord.

The order of readings for Sundays and solemnities extends for a period of three years. Each year within that period is marked with a

[1] GIRM, no. 318.
[2] Introduction to the Lectionary for Mass [= ILM], January 21, 1981, no. 60.
[3] SC, no. 24.
[4] ILM, no. 63.

letter—A, B, or C. The year 1998 is a C year, and so are all years that are multiples of three.

For weekdays, the cycle is only for two years, designated I and II, for odd and even years. Each of these cycles (for Sundays and for weekdays) runs its course independently of the other.[5] This arrangement provides texts for every day of the week throughout the year.

Proper readings are given for celebrations of the saints. In some cases, the readings correspond to biblical passages that mention the saint (as in the case of St. Barnabas, St. Martha, etc.) or about the event in the saint's life that the Mass is celebrating. Other cases feature accommodated readings that bring out some particular aspects of a saint's spiritual life or apostolate. These accommodated readings may take the place of the weekday readings in some instances. However, because the first concern of the priest is the spiritual benefit of the faithful, he is always careful not to impose his personal preference on them. Above all, he is recommended not to omit too often or needlessly the readings assigned for each day in the weekday Lectionary.[6]

IF WE want to know why there are readings in the Mass, we would have to delve into the most ancient of Christian customs. In fact, we would have to go even beyond them to practices dear to the heart of devout Israel. The service of the Jewish synagogue knew such readings from the Law and the Prophets. Have we not seen Jesus reading Isaiah to his fellow Jews (Lk 4:16, 21)? And did not St. Paul, while on his missionary journeys, take part in similar readings (Acts 13:14, 16)?

The early Church faithfully preserved this custom; readings from the sacred books loomed large in the primitive liturgies. In bygone days, these readings had been chosen by the bishop, who also determined their number and length. When he thought that a lesson had lasted long enough, he stopped the reader by saying, "*Deo gratias*" (Thanks be to God). Other lessons followed until the bishop saw fit to end them.

At a fairly early date, however, the standard number of lessons was fixed at three: the first from the Old Testament, called "the proph-

[5] ILM, no. 65.
[6] ILM, no. 83.

ecy"; the second from that part of the New Testament which contains the writings of the apostles (this was called "the apostle" or "the epistle"); and lastly, a reading from the Gospel.

The first and second readings

Generally we find only one of these readings, but on Sundays and solemnities, we find also a second reading.

In a Mass with a sizable congregation, these readings are always to be done at the lectern.[7] There may be concise introductions before the readings. The style proper to such comments must be simple, faithful to the text, brief, and well prepared to suit the text they introduce.[8]

As in other times when people sat around Jesus, we also sit down now to listen to him speaking through the prophets and the apostles. We choose this bodily position because it seems the most fitting for reflection. As good disciples of the Master, we want to listen with peace and serenity to his words, imitating our Blessed Mother, pondering them in our hearts.

We should listen to the word of God with humility and simplicity, and with much attention, so as not to miss anything. The priest takes extra care not to throw away any particle of the consecrated host because it is the blessed body of our Lord. Likewise, although on a different level, we should not miss any part of these readings.

At times, the texts may seem obscure to us because of our limited understanding; at other times, because of the sublimity or depth of the mysteries of God, or because of the special characteristics of the sacred books: their antiquity, their literary genre which is little known nowadays, the different mentality of the age when they were written, and so forth.

Nevertheless, we can be sure that if we do our best, the Holy Spirit will give us enough capacity to grasp whatever we may need for our sanctification and mission in life. And even if what we have read does not stay in our memory, the word of God has purified and nourished our souls.

We will probably find greater difficulty in understanding the

---

[7] ILM, no. 16.
[8] ILM, no. 15.

readings from the Old Testament. Nonetheless, we should receive them with reverence, because "these books, though they also contain some things which are incomplete and temporary, nevertheless show us true divine pedagogy. These same books, then, give expression to a lively sense of God, contain a store of sublime teachings about God, sound wisdom about human life, and a wonderful treasury of prayers, and in them the mystery of our salvation is present in a hidden way." [9]

At the end of the reading, the reader reminds us that what we have just heard is God's word. The people then answer, "Thanks be to God." With this acclamation, they break the silence they were keeping during the reading and while meditating on what they were hearing.

[9] DV, no. 15.

13. Responsorial Psalm and Acclamation before the Gospel

Alleluia! Victory and glory and power to our God! (Rev 19:1).

The Responsorial Psalm

After the first reading comes the responsorial psalm or the Gradual, an integral part of the liturgy of the word.

It was the custom in the Jewish liturgy that the course of the reading be broken by the recitation of psalms. This helped keep away monotony, while allowing a real participation of the congregation in worship. The chants and psalms found in today's missals preserve this ancient custom. That recitation of psalms is a long-standing practice among the Christians themselves is evident from the testimony of St. Hippolytus and Tertullian in the third century.[1] In those days, a trained cantor would sing the psalm while the people joined in the *responsum* (response), generally the first line of the psalm or the *Alleluia*. There was also the Gradual, ordinarily composed of words which appropriately referred to the lesson just read; it was begun by a singer standing on the *gradus* (step) of the lectern. To this verse the congregation replied by taking up a refrain. It soon became a custom for the Gradual verse to be sung by a deacon. But toward the end of the sixth century, Pope St. Gregory discontinued this custom, because it led deacons to care for their voices to the detriment of more important duties.[2]

[1] See St. Hippolytus, *Trad. Ad.*, 51s.; Tertullian, *De or.*, c. 27; also St. Augustine, *Enarr. in Ps.*, 119, 1.

[2] The following is the text of the decision made by the Pope at the Roman Council of the year 595: "It has long been the custom of the Roman Church to make singers deacons, and to use them in singing instead of in preaching or committing the care of the poor to them. The result of this has been that, in admitting anyone to Holy Orders, a good voice has been held in much higher regard that an irreproachable character. Therefore the deacons shall sing nothing in the church except for the Gospel of the Mass. The other lessons shall be sung by the sub-deacons or one of the minor orders" (Quoted in F. Mourret, *L'église et le monde barbare*).

Under the present regulations, the choice of the psalm depends on the readings. The psalmist or cantor of the psalm sings the verses at the lectern or some other suitable place. The people remain seated.[3]

There are two established ways of singing the psalm after the first reading: responsorially and directly. In responsorial singing, which, as far as possible, is to be given preference, the cantor sings the psalm verse, and the whole congregation joins in by singing the response. In direct singing, there is no response by the community; either the psalmist sings alone as the community listens, or all sing it together. When not sung, the psalm is to be recited in a manner conducive to meditation on the word of God.[4]

The psalm when sung may be taken either from the Lectionary or from the *Graduale Romanum*.[5]

THE CHURCH desires that we have a great esteem for the liturgical chants because they are a sign of our heart's cheerfulness. St. Paul recommends that the faithful gathered waiting for the coming of the Lord sing together psalms, hymns, and spiritual canticles (see Col 3:16). The heart shows its joy by singing. Thus St. Augustine says rightly, "To sing belongs to lovers." There is also the ancient proverb: "One who sings well prays twice." [6]

Perhaps we cannot sing to God as well as we would like to; nevertheless, we can be sure that our Father in heaven looks at things differently. We will do fine if we sing with the simplicity and spontaneity of children—after having rehearsed at least a little.

"What is more pleasing than a psalm? David expresses it well: 'Praise the Lord, for a song of praise is good: let there be praise of our God with gladness and grace.' Yes, a psalm is a blessing on the lips of the people, a hymn in praise of God, the assembly's homage, a general acclamation, a word that speaks for all, the voice of the Church, a confession of faith in song. It is the voice of complete assent, the joy of freedom, a cry of happiness, the echo of gladness. It soothes the temper, distracts from care, lightens the burden of sorrow. It is a source of security at night, a lesson in wisdom by day. It is a shield

[3] GIRM, no. 36.
[4] ILM, nos. 20 and 22.
[5] GIRM, no. 36.
[6] GIRM, no. 19.

when we are afraid, a celebration of holiness, a vision of serenity, a promise of peace and harmony. It is like a lyre, evoking harmony from a blend of notes. Day begins to the music of a psalm. Day closes to the echo of a psalm." [7]

After reading this, don't you think that, very often, we can draw our "password," that is, our "aspiration for the day," from the responsorial psalm of the Mass? That "password" will then be liturgical and it will give our day a more supernatural tone.

The *Alleluia*

After the second reading (if there is any), the acclamation before the Gospel or *Alleluia* follows. Unlike the responsorial psalm, it is not related to the preceding reading but to the Gospel which follows. It serves as the assembled faithful's greeting of welcome to the Lord, who is about to speak to them, and as an expression of their faith through song. The whole congregation stands up to sing it. [8]

The word *Alleluia* is an old Judaic expression of joy; it means "praise the Lord." It was incorporated into the liturgy of the Church at a very early date and passed from religion into everyday life. Sailors, when they recognized another ship, used to greet each other with a shout of "*Alleluia*." In the year 429, when the Breton Christians fought the Saxons, they used *Alleluia* as their war cry. St. Jerome heard the farm laborers of Bethlehem sing it while ploughing.

The *Alleluia* was at first sung at Rome only once a year—on Easter Sunday. The historian Sozomen records for us a proverb current in Rome in the fifth century: "God grant that I may hear the *Alleluia*!" This wish is similar to that which we make on New Year's Eve, that we shall again be gathered and reunited as a family at the beginning of the next year. After Easter Sunday, the *Alleluia* was heard during the fifty days of the Easter season.

Nowadays the *Alleluia* is sung in every liturgical season outside Lent. It is usually begun by the cantor or choir, and then it may be repeated by all. The verse which follows is taken from the Lectionary or from the *Graduale*. It ends with a renewed *Alleluia* acclamation from the congregation.

[7] St. Ambrose, *On the Psalms*, 1.9–12; CSEL 64:7:9–10.
[8] ILM, no. 23.

The *Alleluia* is the song of men set free by God, our loving Father;
men redeemed by the blood of Christ. This triumphal acclamation is
linked to the cheerfulness of Easter. "Cheerfulness is a necessary
consequence of our divine filiation, of knowing that our Father God
loves us with a love of predilection, that he holds us up and helps us
and forgives us.

"Remember this and never forget it: even if it should seem at
times that everything around you is collapsing, in fact nothing is collapsing at all, because God does not lose battles." [9]

The Lenten acclamations. During Lent, instead of *Alleluia*, an acclamation is made before and after the verse before the Gospel. The
forms customary for this acclamation are:

Praise to you, Lord Jesus Christ, king of endless glory!
Praise and honor to you, Lord Jesus Christ!
Glory and praise to you, Lord Jesus Christ!
Glory to you, Word of God, Lord Jesus Christ! [10]

The Sequence

In the early liturgy, the singing of the *Alleluia* was extended with a
long vocalization executed on the final vowel, resembling—the
comparison was made by St. Augustine—the joyful modulations of
country people who, without using words, hum a tune on one isolated syllable. This was called the *jubilus*. In the West, words were
put in place of the vocalization of the *jubilus*. The texts which followed the official verses were called "Sequences." Only four of these
beautiful Sequences have been retained.[11] The Sequence is like an
appendix or complement for the *Alleluia*, but it is compulsory only
on Easter Sunday and the day of Pentecost.

---

9 J. Escrivá de Balaguer, *The Forge* (London: Scepter, 1988), no. 332.
10 ILM, no. 91.
11 The four Sequences retained in the Roman Missal are: for Easter, *Victimae Pas-
chali laudes*, a paschal dialogue between the cantor and the congregation; for Pentecost,
Veni Sancti Spiritus, a real masterpiece; for the feast of the Body and Blood of our Lord,
the *Lauda Sion*, a noble page of theology authored by St. Thomas Aquinas; for the celebration of our Lady of Sorrows, *Stabat Mater*, by Jacopone di Todi.

14. The Proclamation of the Gospel

"All authority in heaven and on earth has been given to me. Go, therefore, make disciples of all nations; baptize them in the name of the Father and of the Son and of the Holy Spirit, and teach them to observe all the commands I gave you. And know that I am with you always; yes, to the end of time" (Mt 28:18–20).

The reading of the Gospel is the high point of the liturgy of the word. It is surrounded with special marks of respect. This rite emphasizes the union between the Incarnate Word, the Second Person of the Blessed Trinity, symbolized by the altar and sacramentally present after the Consecration, and the word of God written in the Gospel.

It is a common knowledge that among all the Scriptures, even those of the New Testament, the Gospels have a special preeminence, and rightly so, for they are the principal witness for the life and teaching of the Incarnate Word, our Savior. The Church has always and everywhere held and continues to hold that the four Gospels are of apostolic origin. For what the apostles preached in fulfillment of the commission of Christ, afterward they themselves and apostolic men, under the inspiration of the divine Spirit, handed on to us in writing: the foundation of faith, namely, the fourfold Gospel, according to Matthew, Mark, Luke, and John.[1]

Preparation for the solemn reading

If incense is used, the priest puts some into the censer. Meanwhile, the faithful express to God their cheerfulness by means of the *Alleluia*.

---

[1] DV, no. 18.

Then the deacon who is to proclaim the Gospel bows before the priest and in a low voice asks the blessing:

Father, give me your blessing.

The priest says in a low voice:

The Lord be in your heart and on your lips
that you may worthily proclaim his gospel.
In the name of the Father, and of the Son, and of the Holy Spirit.

If there is no deacon, the priest, with hands joined, bows before the altar and inaudibly says the prayer,

Almighty God, cleanse my heart and my lips
that I may worthily proclaim your gospel.

In less solemn celebrations the priest himself may proclaim all the readings at the lectern and there also, if necessary, the chants between the readings. He bows (usually toward the altar) and says the preceding prayer.

The priest, who is about to speak in Christ's name, prepares himself for that awesome task by begging God to purify his lips as he once did those of Isaiah when an angel touched the great prophet's mouth with a burning coal. This is one of the few prayers during the Mass which the priest says in his own name so that he may exercise his ministry with attention and devotion.[2] We, too, reflect on God's mercy in calling us—improbable people like us—to be Christians, to hear and to proclaim the Gospel. Every Christian preaches Christ every day by the life he lives, by the words he utters from day to day. We are all the time unconsciously influencing other people. Can we say we are doing it worthily?

The reading of the Gospel

If the Book of the Gospels is on the altar, the priest (or deacon) takes it and goes to the lectern. He who is going to read the Gospel may be preceded by servers, who carry the censer and candles. When this little procession reaches the lectern, the priest opens the book and says,

[2] GIRM, no. 13.

The Lord be with you.

Then he introduces:

A reading from the holy gospel according to . . .

The people respond,

Glory to you, Lord.

He makes the sign of the cross with his thumb on the book and on his forehead, mouth, and breast. If incense is used, he incenses the book before reading.[3]

You probably have heard of all the care which, in the centuries before the advent of printing, the Church gave to the calligraphy of Gospel Books, their pages being ornamented with illuminations and their bindings at times encrusted with gold, ivory, and precious stones. The scent of incense used to fill the whole church, and candles were lit "as when," wrote St. Jerome, "the sun shines with all its brilliance; but their flame is not intended to dispel darkness, it is a sign of joy."[4]

We understand why the reading of the Gospel should be done with veneration. Ever since the Gospel was first read in Christian churches, the faithful have never listened to it in any other way than standing. In the Middle Ages, even those leaning on staves would leave them on the ground, standing erect as a servant stands before his lord. The bishop would hold his crozier in hand, and knights would draw their swords from their sheaths, removing also their cloaks and gloves. Men would remove their headgear, and princes their crowns.

Throughout the ages, all present made the sign of the cross together with the priest. Many times also during the day, the first Christians did it with one finger on the forehead. As Tertullian wrote,

Whenever they enter or leave the house, when dressing, when bathing, when about to eat, when lighting the lamps,

[3] GIRM, no. 95.
[4] *Contra Vigilantium,* 8. Quoted in *Dictionnaire d'Archéologie Chretienne et de Liturgie,* 5.1:777.

when going to bed, on rising, on all occasions, they trace the
sign of the cross on their foreheads.

These are signs of special veneration: on the part of the priest or deacon, the blessing and the preparatory prayer, as well as the kiss with
which he concludes the reading; on the part of the faithful, their
standing up and the acclamations with which they acknowledge the
presence of Christ, speaking through these readings.

The Gospel Book is the only book which is incensed, and on
which the sign of the cross is made. It should be read and meditated
on often. We should even memorize, not all its text perhaps, but at
least the most notable passages. "Blessed are they that hear the word
of God and keep it." On hearing the words of the Gospel, our heart
should keep itself prepared, alert, open, and docile. Prepared for
everything? . . . We stand up when reading the Gospel, with the
attitude of one who is prepared to suffer everything for the sake of
those sacred words . . .

> Prepared to die? . . . If necessary, yes!
>
> Prepared to die to ourselves, to our disorderly inclina-
> tions, to our own will? Yes. And that is how you must be
> every day, every moment of every day. . . .
>
> That is how you must be, without the slightest delay or
> hesitation.
>
> That is how you must be: not in the least half-hearted,
> without the slightest complaint.
>
> That is how you must be: doing everything, giving every-
> thing, giving yourself, with your heart generously opened
> wide, manfully and *cheerfully*: Bread given grudgingly never
> tastes good to the poor. . . . The apostle said, "God loves
> the cheerful giver."
>
> You will ask: Everything, Lord? This, yes, I will sacrifice
> it to you. But that other thing, Lord, . . . it is so hard to
> give it up.
>
> Can the Lord, who is so good, ask me to sacrifice this
> desire, this legitimate wish, this holy affection?
>
> Can he not ask me to make other sacrifices, perhaps
> greater ones than this?

Fix your eyes on the crucifix and listen to what I have to say to you: Everything, everything . . . your most legitimate desires, your most holy ambitions, those occupations of yours which you carry out with the highest supernatural motives. Look: The best thing for you is to do *that thing* which he asks of you, in the *way* he asks for it, in the *place* where he asks for it. Give him *that* . . . without hesitation.[5]

The end of the reading

When the priest has finished the reading, he says,

The gospel of the Lord.

We unanimously answer,

Praise to you, Lord Jesus Christ.

With this, we make a firm resolution to apply to our lives the teachings we have just received, giving to Christ our entire lives—lest he tell us, "Why do you call me 'Lord, Lord,' and not do what I say?" (Lk 6:46).

Until the thirteenth century, the Book of the Gospels was brought to be kissed by the clergy and even by the faithful. Nowadays, only the priest who has just read the Gospel kisses it.

We can at least make ours the kiss the priest has placed on the sacred book. With it, we want to tell our Lord we are ready to give our lives for the truths contained in the Gospel. At the same time, we ask forgiveness for our faults, interiorly accompanying the celebrant who, while kissing the book, says,

May the words of the gospel wipe away our sins.

---

[5] Bernard Vasconcelos, *Your Mass*, pp. 42–43.

15. Homily

Make use of the time until I arrive by reading to the people, preaching and teaching. You have in you a spiritual gift which was given to you . . . when they laid their hands on you; do not let it lie unused (1 Tim 4:13–14).

On certain days, the homily follows the proclamation of the Gospel. It is an integral part of the liturgy. It is said that the ideal homily is firmly based on the readings of the Mass, is not too long (7–10 minutes), and sticks to the subject.[1]

In the synagogue, the Bible readings were always followed by an explanation of the sacred text. Our Lord took advantage of such instances to announce the kingdom of God (see Mk 1:21 and Lk 4:16ff.). This custom was observed also in the primitive Church. The bishop himself, who normally celebrated the Mass on Sundays, spoke to the congregation. This was one of his main duties. We keep precious texts of homilies from St. John Chrysostom, St. Augustine, and even from popes like St. Leo the Great and St. Gregory the Great. They always took from the Scriptures the themes for the instruction of the faithful and made good use of scriptural passages in tackling points of dogma and morals.

Homily means "explanation" in Greek. Its purpose is to develop, explain, and teach the way of transforming into life what has been proclaimed. Accordingly, the homily is to be given by the priest or the deacon.[2] No lay person is allowed to preside over this means of catechesis.

---

[1] In *On the Instruction of the Ingenuous*, St. Augustine declares that he had noticed that during the sermon, some yawned and others scarcely concealed their desire to be off. So he advises, whenever signs of tiredness are noticeable, the preacher to divert the people with an anecdote or with a moving story which would reawaken their attention. But, he adds, above all, shorten the discourse. "If you wish to cure their boredom, be sparing with the medicine. Hurry, promise that you will soon finish, and finish very quickly."

[2] Sacred Congregation for the Sacraments and Divine Worship, Instruction *Inaestimabile Donum* [= ID] on Certain Norms Concerning Worship of the Eucharistic Mystery, April 17, 1980, no. 3.

The homily usually dwells on some point of the readings or of another text from the Ordinary or from the Proper prayers of the Mass of the day, so that it becomes alive for us here and now. It takes into account the mystery being celebrated and the needs of the listeners. The mysteries of the faith and the guiding principles of Christian life are expounded during the course of the liturgical year.[3]

The importance and the source of this healthy nourishment for the intellect is pointed out in the recent documents of the Magisterium. We are told that:

> Catechesis should always draw its content from the living source of the word of God transmitted in Tradition and the Scriptures, as from a single sacred deposit. It must be impregnated and penetrated by the thought, the spirit and the outlook of the Bible and the Gospels through constant contact with the texts themselves; but also, catechesis should be all the richer and more effective by reading the texts with the understanding and the heart of the Church and by drawing inspiration from the two thousand years of the Church's reflection and life.[4]

The writings of the holy Doctors of the Church, of so many saints, are a treasure chest from which abundant inspiration can be drawn.

> Indeed the homily is supremely suitable for the use of such texts, provided that their content corresponds to the required conditions, since it is one of the tasks that belong to the nature of the homily to show the points of convergence between revealed divine wisdom and noble human thought seeking the truth by various paths.[5]

It is advisable to stress the essential subordination of the liturgy of the word to the eucharistic liturgy during the homily. Then, the commentary on the scriptural texts becomes like a preparation for the Consecration and the Communion.

[3] SC, no. 52; GIRM, no. 41.
[4] John Paul II, Apostolic Exhortation *Catechesi Tradendae* on Catechesis in Our Time, October 16, 1979, no. 27.
[5] DC, no. 10.

The homily should never be omitted on Sundays and holy days of obligation; and it is strongly recommended on other days, especially on the weekdays of Advent, Lent, and the Easter season.[6]

In order that it might more effectively move men's minds, the priest should explain the word of God not in a general and abstract way, but rather by applying the lasting truth of the Gospel to the particular circumstances of life.[7]

The task is not an easy one for the priest, though. For he has to try to apply the Gospel's doctrine to real life, without mixing private viewpoints or personal opinions, even involuntarily.

To avoid that risk, the priest always tries to lead all and each one to unity in charity and to the development of one's own vocation. He tries to harmonize different mentalities so that no one feels like a stranger in the community of the faithful. In building the Christian community, priests are never to put themselves at the service of some human faction or ideology. Rather, they are to respect in the faithful that freedom with which Christ has made us free.[8]

Lay people, on the other hand, should correspond to the effort and zeal of the priest preaching the homily. They should not mind the obvious limitations and imperfections which accompany any human instrument. Rarely will a homily leave satisfied those who are shallow and mean. But it will always profit those who go to the essentials, while understanding and overlooking the human shortcomings of the preacher.

[6] GIRM, no. 41.
[7] PO, no. 4.
[8] PO, no. 6.

16. The Creed or Profession of Faith

It is impossible to please God without faith, since anyone who comes to him must believe that he exists and rewards those who try to find him (Heb 11:6).

All that Christ has come to teach us, we do believe with all the strength of our soul. Such is the summary of the Creed. The symbol or Creed expresses our response and assent to what we have just heard in the readings and in the homily. In the liturgy of the word, the Word of God, now Incarnate, has spoken to men. He will come to offer himself upon the altar in the liturgy of the Eucharist. The Creed thus becomes a wonderful link between these two parts of the Mass.

OUR Creed was not drawn up for use at Mass. In the earliest days of Christianity, a profession of faith was a prerequisite for being baptized. No doubt, the formula was quite simple, something perhaps like the profession of faith made by the Ethiopian eunuch to Philip before baptism, when he said, "I believe that Jesus Christ is the Son of God" (Acts 8:37). That explains why in the Apostles' Creed (as well as in the original Latin text of the Creed of the Mass) we speak in the singular: "I believe . . ."

From this usage in the baptismal liturgy, the Creed later became an instrument to curb the heresy that threatened the principles of the faith. There arose the need to state these principles in precise and definite terms. The symbols of the faith contained the concrete propositions of belief in brief affirmations. However, the familiar statements of the Apostles' Creed did not measure up to the degree of precision needed. So a more elaborate statement of belief or Creed was drawn up at the Council of Chalcedon (A.D. 451). It combined the truths of the faith professed by the two earlier councils, one held in Nicaea (325), the other at Constantinople (381). It is this Nicene-Constantinopolitan Creed, basically, that we find in our Sunday Masses.

Furthermore, there were open questions then about the Three Persons of the Blessed Trinity. In the climate of doctrinal unrest in the fourth century, a heretic could easily steal into the assembly of the faithful. How might this insult to the holy mysteries be prevented, except by compelling the whole congregation to state the Catholic faith and affirm their adherence to it?

Such usage of the Creed in the liturgy began in Antioch and Constantinople. Then it spread to Spain, where it was adopted in the Council of Toledo (589). The council specified that the Creed should be recited before the Lord's Prayer: "Let the Creed resound, so that the true faith may be declared in song, and that the souls of believers, in accepting that faith, may be ready to partake, in Communion, of the body and blood of Christ." [1]

The Creed thus became, together with the Lord's Prayer, a preparation for Communion. From Spain, it passed to Western Europe, where it was placed after the Gospel. Rome itself did not adopt it in the Mass until the year 1014. [2]

NOWADAYS, the Profession of Faith by the priest and the people is obligatory on Sundays and solemnities. It may be said also at special, more solemn celebrations. [3]

We can distinguish three parts in the Creed:

A confession of faith in God, the Father, our Creator, maker of heaven and earth, of all that is seen and unseen.

A confession of faith in Christ, our Lord. He is God, who by the power of the Spirit became incarnate from the Virgin Mary and was made man. (At these words, all bow as a sign of reverence for the mystery.) Then we focus on Christ's passion and death on the cross; his resurrection, ascension, and participation in the judg-

---

[1] Council of Toledo (A.D. 589), can. 2 (Mansi 9:993). The Creed is still prayed before the Lord's Prayer in the Mozarabic rite, sometimes used in Spain. In our time, it has been reintroduced before the Lord's Prayer in the initiation of catechumens (see *Ordo Initiationis Christianae Adultorum*, 25–26, 183–187).

[2] It is said that a very spirited Roman answered criticisms by retorting that inasmuch as Rome had never fallen into heresy, the recitation of the Creed in the Mass was unnecessary there.

[3] GIRM, no. 44.

ment to reign forever, as it was announced by the angel to the Virgin Mary (Lk 1:33).

A confession of faith in the means of salvation, supplied by God, the Holy Spirit, the giver of supernatural life. We declare how he works through the Church.

We believe in one holy, catholic, and apostolic Church. *Catholic* means "universal"—a reminder that the Church exists throughout the world and embraces the *entire* revelation of God. Those who accepted only a part of it were called heretics (from *hairesis*, "to take a choice," "to join a sect"). The Church is *apostolic* because she traces her origins back to Christ through the apostles and always teaches the message the apostles received from him.

At an early period of history (*c.* A.D. 350), St. Cyril, Bishop of Jerusalem, described the catholicity of the one Church with the following words:

> The Church is called Catholic or universal because it has spread throughout the entire world, from one end of the earth to the other. Again, it is called Catholic because it teaches fully and unfailingly all the doctrines which ought to be brought to men's knowledge, whether concerned with visible or invisible things, with the realities of heaven or the things of earth. Another reason for the name Catholic is that the Church brings under religious obedience all classes of men, rulers and subjects, learned and unlettered. Finally, it deserves the title Catholic because it heals and cures unrestrictedly every type of sin that can be committed in soul or in body, and because it possesses within itself every kind of virtue that can be named, whether exercised in actions or in words or in some kind of spiritual charism.[4]

The Church is continually sanctified by the Holy Spirit; thus, all those who believe have access through Christ to God the Father.[5] She transmits that salvation by means of the sacraments,[6] real channels of

[4] *Catecheses*, 18, 23: PG 33:1043.
[5] LG, no. 4.
[6] LG, no. 11.

grace. Since the Creed was once said immediately before baptism, it is natural that it includes a statement of belief in "one baptism for the forgiveness of sins."

We end up declaring that our future resurrection is on the way to our final coronation as new creatures.

THE Creed is none other than the marvelous history of God's love for us. That this truth necessarily surpasses our understanding should not astonish us. Can we pretend to comprehend the infinity of God and the immensity of his purposes in human words and thoughts?

In these times of doctrinal confusion, we should be careful not to compromise the content of our faith, not even in small things. "If we give up in any point of the Christian dogma, it will be necessary to yield in another, and then in another, and thus until such concessions become normal and licit. And once we have set ourselves in motion to reject the dogma bit by bit, what will happen at the end, but to repudiate it in its entirety?" [7]

It is worthwhile putting our lives on the line, giving ourselves completely, so as to respond to the love and the confidence that God has placed in us. It is worthwhile, above all, to decide to take our Christian life seriously. When we recite the Creed, we state that we believe in God the Father Almighty, in his Son, Jesus Christ, who died and rose again, and in the Holy Spirit, the Lord and giver of life. We affirm that the Church—one, holy, catholic, and apostolic—is the body of Christ enlivened by the Holy Spirit. We rejoice in the forgiveness of sins and in the hope of the resurrection.

But do those words penetrate to the depths of our own heart? Or do they remain only on our lips? The divine message of victory, the joy and the peace of Pentecost, should be the unshakeable foundation of every Christian's way of thinking and acting and living.[8]

---

[7] St. Vincent of Lerins, *Commonitorium*, no. 23.
[8] J. Escrivá de Balaguer, *Christ Is Passing By*, no. 129.

17. General Intercessions or Prayer of the Faithful

Holy Father, keep those you have given me true to your name, so that they may be one like us. I am not asking you to remove them from the world, but to protect them from the Evil One. I pray not only for these, but for those also who through their words will believe in me (Jn 17:11, 15, 20).

In the General Intercessions or Prayer of the Faithful, the congregation prays for the needs of the Church and the world, responding to the invitation made by the celebrant.

As a rule, this is the sequence of intentions:

For the needs of the Church: for the pope, the bishops, the shepherds of souls; for the missions, the unity of Christians, vocations, etc.

For public authorities and the salvation of the world: for peace among nations, rulers, development of people, social justice; for a bountiful harvest; for freedom, prosperity, etc.

For those oppressed by any need: for the poor, the persecuted; for the sick, broken homes, the jobless; for those in jail, unbelievers; for those who doubt, etc.

For the local community: including the deceased, the absent, the destitute; the dying; the clergy, the families; the newlywed couples, etc.

We make these intentions our own either by silent prayer or by a response said together after each intention, such as these:

Lord, hear our prayer.

Lord, have mercy.

In England and Wales, following a very old tradition, the petitions are followed by a beautiful prayer to our Lady, the Hail Mary.

We end the Prayer of the Faithful with the concluding prayer said by the priest, asking God to accept our petitions.

With this, the liturgy of the word comes to an end.

To PRAY for the needs of the Church and of the world is an early Christian custom. St. Paul admonishes Timothy, one of his disciples:

> My advice is that, first of all, there should be prayers offered for everyone—petitions, intercessions and thanksgiving—and especially for kings and others in authority, so that we may be able to live religious and reverent lives in peace and quiet (1 Tim 2:1–3).

St. Justin, in A.D. 150, bears witness to the existence of this part of the Mass in his time:

> After the homily of the bishop we all stand and raise our prayers . . . for our own selves, for those who have been just lighted up [baptized], and for all the rest, found elsewhere.[1]

The people responded with *Kyrie eleison* (Lord, have mercy) or any other invocation. The bishop intervened just at the end to say the final prayer.[2]

LAY PERSONS fulfill their vocation in the middle of the world by transforming it according to Gospel values. Therefore, we must love all honest environments and situations of human life. "The world awaits us. Yes, we love the world passionately because God has taught us to: *Sic Deus dilexit mundum* . . .—God so loved the world. And we love it because it is there that we fight our battles in a most beautiful war of charity, so that everyone may find the peace that Christ has come to establish."[3] There, we will be able to make present and operative the new life that flows from the redemption

---

[1] St. Justin, *Apol.*, 1, 65, 67.

[2] A. Jungmann, *Missarum Sollemnia*, no. 619.

[3] J. Escrivá de Balaguer, *Furrow* (New York: Scepter, 1987), no. 290.

only if we remain deeply rooted in the eucharistic memorial of Christ's sacrifice.

All of us gathered in the temple stir up our priestly heart to intercede for the salvation of all and for all their needs, spiritual as well as material. Thus, we will be ready to spread the whole message of salvation, "keeping in mind the true meaning of ethics in which the distinction between good and evil is not relativized, the real meaning of sin, the necessity for conversion, and the universality of the law of fraternal love." [4] "If, like some people, we were to think that to keep a clean heart, a heart worthy of God, means 'not mixing it up, not contaminating it' with human affection, we would become insensitive to other people's pain and sorrow. We would be capable only of an 'official charity,' something dry and soulless.

"A man or a society that does not react to suffering and injustice and makes no effort to alleviate them is still distant from the love of Christ's heart. While Christians enjoy the fullest freedom in finding and applying various solutions to these problems, they should be united in having one and the same desire to serve mankind. Otherwise their Christianity will not be the word and life of Jesus; it will be a fraud, a deception of God and man." [5]

The law of fraternal love is a consequence of our divine filiation. All those who are called to share the same faith are brothers, children of the same Father. We realize we cannot enclose ourselves in an exclusively individualistic search for God. Each one must commit himself to help the others get closer to God and to give an answer to the present needs of the world. "A man who does not love the brother that he can see cannot love God, whom he has never seen" (1 Jn 4:20). Each one must be ready to serve the others, helping to find solutions to their problems and to unjust situations.

However, we are reminded that:

An effective defense of justice needs to be based on the truth of mankind, created in the image of God and called to the grace of divine sonship. The recognition of the true

---

[4] Sacred Congregation for the Doctrine of the Faith, *Instruction on Certain Aspects of the "Theology of Liberation"* (August 6, 1984), XI, no. 17.

[5] J. Escrivá de Balaguer, *Christ Is Passing By*, no. 167.

relationship of human beings to God constitutes the foundation of justice to the extent that it rules the relationships between people. That is why the fight for the rights of man, which the Church does not cease to reaffirm, constitutes the authentic fight for justice.

The truth of mankind requires that this battle be fought in ways consistent with human dignity.

The acute need for radical reforms of the structures which conceal poverty and which are themselves forms of violence, should not let us lose the fact that the source of injustice is the hearts of men. Therefore it is only by making an appeal to the *moral potential* of the person and to the constant need for interior conversion, that social change will be brought about which will truly be in the service of man.[6]

---

[6] *Instruction on Certain Aspects of the "Theology of Liberation,"* XI, nos. 6–8.

PART IV
LITURGY OF THE EUCHARIST

As Christ Commanded in the Upper Room

A. The Preparation of the Gifts

In the Last Supper, our Lord Jesus Christ, anticipating the sacrifice of the cross, gave us the blueprint of the Mass. An early account by St. Paul tells us how Christ's command to perpetuate the sacrifice was carried out by the first Christians:

> For this is what I received from the Lord, and in turn passed on to you: that on the same night that he was betrayed, the Lord Jesus took some bread, and thanked God for it and broke it, and he said, "This is my body, which is for you; do this as a memorial of me." In the same way he took the cup after supper, and said, "This cup is the new covenant in my blood. Whenever you drink it, do this as a memorial of me." Until the Lord comes, therefore, every time you eat this bread and drink this cup, you are proclaiming his death (1 Cor 11:23–26).

And this is precisely what takes place during the liturgy of the Eucharist. The sacrifice of the cross is continuously present in the Church when the priest, representing Christ the Lord, carries out what the Lord did and commanded his disciples to do in his memory. We can identify three steps in the liturgy of the Eucharist:

The Preparation of the Gifts. The bread and wine with water, the elements that Christ used, are brought to the altar.

The Eucharistic Prayer. The Church gives thanks to God for the whole work of salvation and the gifts of bread and wine become the body and blood of Christ.

Communion Rite. Through the breaking of the bread, the unity of the faithful is expressed; and through Communion,

they receive the Lord's body and blood in the same way that
the apostles received Communion from Christ's own
hands.[1]

---

[1] GIRM, no. 48.

18. *Gifts Are Brought*

May the contrite soul, the humbled spirit be as acceptable to you as holocausts of rams and bullocks, as thousands of fattened lambs: such let our sacrifice be to you today, and may it be your will that we follow you wholeheartedly, since those who put their trust in you will not be disappointed (Dan 3:39–40).

At the beginning of the liturgy of the Eucharist, the gifts, which will become Christ's body and blood, are brought to the altar.

First, the altar, the Lord's table, which is the center of the entire eucharistic liturgy, is prepared: The corporal, purificator, missal, and chalice are placed on it. The gifts are then brought forward.[1] While the priest receives the offerings, the offertory song is sung; otherwise, it is omitted.

This rite is described by St. Justin (second century) with stark impersonal simplicity: "Bread, water, and wine are brought." The first Christians had no special ceremonies accompanying this rite, for it was their desire to depart from pagan sacrificial practices. At the same time, they emphasized the special character of the Victim, which is not the bread and wine, but our Lord himself.

However, later on, it became necessary to defend the intrinsic goodness of created things against Gnosticism, while making it clear that the gifts brought to the altar are not the Victim to be sacrificed. The congregation participated in the act of offering by approaching the altar in procession and presenting various gifts: not only bread and wine, but also other edible items and other things, such as gold and silver, and even flowers. The deacons sorted out these gifts and put aside those that would be used in the Mass. The rest was given to the poor or used for the needs of the Church. During this procession, a chant was sung—a custom that gave birth to the offertory antiphon.

Toward the Middle Ages, this practice disappeared gradually, no doubt because of the risk that it could give way to disorder.

[1] GIRM, no. 49.

Even though the faithful no longer, as in the past, bring the bread and wine for the liturgy from their homes, the rite of carrying the gifts up to the altar retains the same spiritual value and meaning. The participation of the faithful is expressed by their bringing the bread and wine for the celebration of the Eucharist, or other gifts for the needs of the Church and the poor.

The bread and wine that we offer are poor and humble gifts. Yet, precisely for that reason, they aptly represent our smallness before God. However, because of the eucharistic *transubstantiation*, we will actually be offering to God not these lowly tokens of our creature-hood, but his only begotten Son, the only Victim worthy of him. The offering of bread and wine, gifts in kind, money, and so on, and even that of our own person, derives all its value from union with the divine Victim. This Victim, offered by us and for us, will absorb our own oblation.

Together with Christ, we offer everything that we are and all that we possess, all that we have done or try to do. We offer our memory, intelligence, and will; our family, profession, hobbies, success, suffer-ings, failures, and worries; and our aspirations and spiritual commun-ions. Likewise, we offer our small and big mortifications: all those acts of love we performed yesterday and as many as we plan to per-form today. "The appropriate word you left unsaid; the joke you didn't tell; the cheerful smile for those who bother you; that silence when you're unjustly accused; your kind conversation with people you find boring and tactless; the daily effort to overlook one irritat-ing detail or another in those who live with you . . ." [2]

But let us not forget to offer also the happy events and the pleas-ant things that mark our day and our entire life. Do not think that God likes our sufferings more than our joys. No. What he really likes is the constancy of our love, whatever happens to us. He is our Father, and he enjoys seeing how we try to overcome the disor-der sin brought into the world. We achieve victory by fighting against the enemies of our soul: from within, our concupiscence, attachments, and pride; from without, the devil, the world, and the flesh.

---

[2] J. Escrivá de Balaguer, *The Way*, no. 173.

When our Lord called the first apostles they were busy
mending their broken nets by the side of an old boat. Our
Lord told them to follow him and *statim*—immediately—
they left everything—*relictis omnibus*—everything! And followed him.

Sometimes, though we wish to imitate them, we find we
don't manage to leave everything, and there remains some
attachment in our heart, something wrong in our life which
we're not willing to break with and offer it up to God.

Won't you examine your heart in depth? Nothing should
remain there except what is his. If not, we aren't loving
him, neither you nor I. [3]

God is also happy to see our dreams come true, our goals conquered,
our business running well—in a word, seeing how we love everything he sends us. "If things go well let's rejoice, blessing God who
makes them prosper. And if they go wrong? Let's rejoice, blessing
God, who allows us to share the sweetness of his cross." [4]

Obviously, we cannot correspond adequately with our gifts for
everything we have received from the Lord of heaven and earth.
Nevertheless, our gifts are a token of our sincere desire to restore
God's dominion over creation, disrupted by sin. This is the work of
redemption, performed by Christ, but to be completed by each of us.
The offertory song is like the smile that accompanies a gift and
makes it more pleasing to the receiver. "God loves the cheerful
giver" (2 Cor 9:7). And our gift to Christ is the desire to participate
with him in the sacrifice of the cross, overcoming the passions that
tend to pull us down, especially the fear of giving ourselves in total
self-surrender.

At the offertory, let us tell our Lord: "I have no use for divided
hearts. I give mine whole and not in parts." [5] For Love has to be
repaid with love.

[3] J. Escrivá de Balaguer, *The Forge*, no. 356.
[4] Escrivá, *The Forge*, no. 658.
[5] Escrivá, *The Forge*, no. 145.

19. From Many Grains, from Many Grapes

Melchisedech king of Salem brought bread and wine; he was a priest of God Most High. He pronounced this blessing: "Blessed be Abram by God Most High, creator of heaven and earth, and blessed be God Most High for handing over your enemies to you" (Gen 14:18–20).

Offering of the bread

The priest, standing at the altar, takes the paten with the bread and, holding it slightly raised above the altar, says,

Blessed are you, Lord, God of all creation.
Through your goodness we have this bread to offer,
which earth has given and human hands have made.
It will become for us the bread of life.

We may respond, "Blessed be God for ever."

THE FIRST Christians used ordinary bread at Mass, but it was of the best available, marked with a cross or some other symbol of Christ. From about the ninth century, *azyme* bread began to be used, recalling the unleavened bread Jesus used at the Last Supper.[1]

The more we think about it, the clearer it becomes: God could not have chosen anything simpler to symbolize our personal surrender to him. Bread is the most eloquent symbol of human existence. To earn your bread means to make a living. Are we mistaken in discovering in this sacramental medium our Lord's intention of linking the Holy Eucharist to the most humble of our life's activities?

---

[1] We call hosts the pieces of unleavened bread for Communion. Originally, "host" (from Latin *hostire*, to strike) referred to any animal about to be sacrificed. Hence, among some orientals, it is called "the lamb," and also "the seal," for it carried a sign or mark. On the other hand, the consecrated host is called "the First Born" and "the Blazing Coal," among them.

The little piece of bread on the paten represents, poetically, the union of man's work with the earth, a natural element. "There is no scrap of bread which does not call to mind the hard work of ploughing and sowing, the moist brow of the reaper, the weariness of the arms which have threshed the corn, and the grunts of the baker who kneaded the dough close to the scorching oven." [2]

Therefore, when we offer bread as a participation in Christ's sacrifice, we intend to offer also all the beauty and goodness of nature united to our own work.

At this moment, we recall the Gospel episode of the multiplication of the loaves and the fish. Here in the Mass, Christ is going to feed, with the food of immortality, all who are willing to accept him. But, as in the Gospel scene, he wants us to put in whatever we have got. The boy in the Gospel parted with the few loaves and fish that he had, even though he could not believe his meager contribution would solve anything. The apostles themselves remarked, "What is that among so many?" (Jn 6:9).

Offering of wine

After he has offered the bread, the celebrant, standing to one side of the altar, pours wine into the chalice, and adds to it a little water, saying,

> By the mystery of this water and wine
> may we come to share in the divinity of Christ,
> who humbled himself to share in our humanity.

We ratify this supplication with a movement of our heart.

The priest goes again to the center of the altar, takes the chalice, and, holding it slightly raised above the altar, says,

> Blessed are you, Lord, God of all creation.
> Through your goodness we have this wine to offer,
> fruit of the vine and work of human hands.
> It will become our spiritual drink.

---

[2] Georges Chevrot, *Our Mass* (Collegeville, Minn.: The Liturgical Press, 1958), p. 98.

Then he places the chalice on the corporal. Bowing in an attitude of profound humility, offering not only these gifts but also our self-oblation, he says,

> Lord God, we ask you to receive us
> and be pleased with the sacrifice we offer you
> with humble and contrite hearts.

This prayer is taken from the song of the three companions of Daniel who were thrown into the furnace (Dan 3:39–40). The priest speaks in his own name and in those of the faithful, and asks God to accept the sacrifice about to be offered. God should find in us true humility and sincere repentance for our sins.

At this moment, the gifts of bread and wine and the altar itself may be incensed—a symbol of the Church's offerings and prayers going up to God. Afterward, the ministers and the people may be incensed, too.[3]

It was an ancient custom to take the wine mixed with water, which the chalice of Jesus in the Last Supper contained. The Church retained this gesture to symbolize the sanctification of the Christian which is accomplished through his union with Jesus Christ. The water becomes the symbol of ourselves: our lives, with our weaknesses.

Have you stopped to think what happens to the drops of water mixed with the wine? They are absorbed by it and then become inseparable from it. So does Jesus absorb us. The drops of water are of negligible worth; they are not even enough to quench anyone's thirst. Yet they will end up being divine blood! And all that because they let themselves be mixed with the wine and be dissolved in it, thus manifesting self-denial, personal renunciation.

At this moment, we grow in our desire to offer ourselves in total self-surrender, as the few drops of water in the chalice have reminded us. So we will be able to become one with Jesus Christ after the Consecration.

[3] GIRM, no. 51.

20. From the Washing of Hands to the Prayer over the Gifts

O God, in your goodness, in your great tenderness wipe away my faults; wash me clean of my guilt, purify me from my sin (Ps 51:1–2).

In every Mass, a liturgical act is performed which originally was a response to a practical necessity. The celebrant *washes his hands*, which have touched the sundry offerings as well as the censer, before taking up the bread about to become the body of Christ. The Church has kept this ceremony of the *Lavabo* to express the desire of interior purification. This mystical meaning was emphasized by St. Cyril of Jerusalem in the fourth century, when he wrote: "This action shows that we must be free from all sin. We perform actions with our hands; to wash our hands is the nearest thing to purifying our deeds." [1]

This is the way the celebrant understands it. To express his desire to be cleansed within, he washes his hands at the side of the altar while he says,

Lord, wash away my iniquity; cleanse me from my sin.

The priest then returns to the center of the altar and begs us to unite ourselves with him in the sacrificial act as it draws nearer. He seems to pause in what he is doing, extending and then joining his hands, to make a last pressing appeal for unity, before he proceeds to the Consecration. He does this by using the words of a medieval prayer which is a sort of long-drawn "Let us pray":

Pray, brethren, that our sacrifice
may be acceptable to God, the almighty Father.

In the original Latin text, the priest stresses that the sacrifice is *mine* (i.e., Christ offers himself—the aspect of ministerial priesthood) *and yours* (the entire Church offers the sacrifice—the aspect of common

---

[1] *Catechesis Mystagogical*, v, 2.

priesthood). Our answer expresses with the same simplicity the intentions of the Mass:

> *May the Lord accept the sacrifice at your hands*
> *for the praise and glory of his name,*
> *for our good, and the good of all his Church.*

The preparation of the gifts concludes with the Prayer over the Gifts that the priest addresses to God in the name of all of us present and the entire holy people.[2] We stand up at this presidential prayer to signify our unity in faith and worship.[3]

In the early ages of Christianity, the processional entrance ended with the Collect; and the distribution of Communion with what we now call Prayer after Communion. Likewise, the presentation of the gifts concluded with the Prayer over the Gifts, which was said in the *orans* attitude, i.e., with arms outstretched.

In the Prayer over the Gifts, we usually acknowledge our incapacity to offer to God gifts adequate to his goodness and power. We ask God to accept what we offer with sincerity. We ask some grace in connection with the mystery celebrated on that particular day, in return for the material gifts. We notice an ascending or upward-striving rhythm in the progress of the liturgical action. If we contrast this prayer with the Collect, we can perceive an increase in fervor and assurance. We know that our gifts to God will be returned to us multiplied a hundredfold.

We should not forget that the only worthy offering is that of the body and blood of Christ. Our inward gift of self to God consists in a life lived in a state of grace; it means fleeing from sin and being faithful to our ordinary duties.

St. Paul exhorted the first Christians to offer every action to God. "Whatever you eat, whatever you drink, whatever you do at all, do it for the glory of God" (1 Cor 10:31), and never say or do anything except "in the name of the Lord Jesus" (Col 3:17). The Second Vatican Council encourages ordinary Christians to make their daily offering united to the eucharistic sacrifice:

---

[2] GIRM, no. 10.
[3] GIRM, no. 21.

For all their works, prayers and apostolic endeavors, their ordinary married and family life, if patiently borne—all these become "spiritual sacrifices acceptable to God through Jesus Christ" (1 Pet 2:5). Together with the offering of the Lord's body, they are most fittingly offered in the celebration of the Eucharist.[4]

Every morning we should offer our day to God. We need not do it always with a concrete formula. This practice of piety, like an anticipated Prayer over the Gifts, will serve as a preparation for the Eucharist. Our *morning offering* will awake our spirit of service, and will guard us against the temptation of pride, love of comfort, and irresponsibility.

[4] LG, no. 34.

PART IV
LITURGY OF THE EUCHARIST (*Continued*)

B. The Eucharistic Prayer

The Eucharistic Prayer marks the summit of the Mass. This does not mean that the other parts of the Mass are less precious. They are important, too. But they find their center and climax in the Eucharistic Prayer.

Eucharist means "thanksgiving." As the priest recites the Eucharistic Prayer, we should concentrate all our senses on the action—the mystery—taking place on the altar. We should join the priest and the entire Church in offering to God the redeeming sacrifice of Christ on the cross, and give thanks for God's goodness and glory.

21. *Prayer, Thanksgiving, Action*

From the farthest east to farthest west my name is honored among the nations and everywhere a sacrifice is offered to my name, and a pure offering too, since my name is honored among the nations, says Yahweh Sabaoth (Mal 1:11).

The Eucharistic Prayer begins with a short dialogue between the priest and us, before the Preface, and ends with the doxology preceding the Lord's Prayer. Throughout the prayer, the priest speaks in the first person plural; he repeatedly says "we," which places him at the head of the body, which is the Church, *in the person of Christ.* Only when he pronounces the words of the Consecration does he slip into the first person singular, as he *puts on Christ* in a unique manner. The other pronoun to notice is "you," addressed to the Father.

This central point of the Mass has received several names in history. Recently, it is usually called the *Eucharistic Prayer,* a name that aptly describes it. The term *Canon,* or *Canon Actionis,* is also used. This word, of Greek origin, means rule or standard. It points out the official text for the most important liturgical action. Hence, the expressions *Liturgical Action* and *Sacred Action* are also applied to the Eucharistic Prayer. So is the word *Anaphora,* which means offering.

It is really so, a *prayer* that the Son of God, with the Church forever united to him, directs to God the Father. The Eucharistic Prayer is Christocentric as well, because it makes constant references to the main actions of the Second Person of the Blessed Trinity, represented by the priest, *the other Christ.*

In the Gospels, the kingdom of God is compared to a wedding feast. Jesus is the bridegroom who loves and gives eternal life to his spouse, the Church, the "bride adorned for her husband" (Rev 21:2). The redemptive act of Christ the Bridegroom toward the Church the Bride is expressed in the Eucharist in a most excellent manner. The Mass then becomes like an anticipation and foretaste of the banquet of heaven.

This fact explains also why women are not to be ordained: Since priesthood is a sacrament, it is a sign that not only is effective but also should be intelligible to the faithful. "When Christ's role in the Eucharist is to be expressed sacramentally, there would not be this 'natural resemblance' which must exist between Christ and his minister if the role of Christ were not taken by a man." [1]

We perceive in the different forms of Eucharistic Prayer clear expressions of praise to God, especially at the beginning. The reason for them is gratefulness, which explains another element in this prayer: *thanksgiving*. All of it is an act of thanksgiving, even though the word *thanks* hardly occurs. Words are not enough to express our feelings when the favor we receive is immeasurable. Perhaps this explains why children refuse to say anything when they receive a gift. Very often, they show their gratefulness with the glint of their eyes or with a kiss. *They give thanks with action, with deeds.*

The Eucharistic Prayer includes not only words but also *action*: the *Consecration*. For this reason, it is the model, root, and crown of the personal prayer of every Christian.

THE HOUR of the sacrifice has come. The celebrant now moves more solemnly than before. All his motions are charged with a consciousness of their meaning as he progresses from action to action, now joining his hands, now raising them to heaven, after having made the sign of the cross over the offerings.

At the beginning of the sixth century, there was in the East a tendency for the priest to say the Canon in seclusion, in order to emphasize the idea of mystery. A partition, called *iconostasis*, adorned with icons, was set between the sanctuary and the people. Although it had windows, this structure hid the altar from the view of the congregation. The celebrant sang the Anaphora straight through.

However, that was not the custom in the Roman rite. The faithful always had the unique privilege of being direct witnesses of the mystery, as St. Caesarius, the Bishop of Arles (in the early sixth century), pointed out: "You can read the prophecies, the epistles, and the

[1] Congregation for the Doctrine of the Faith, Declaration Concerning the Question of the Admission of Women to the Ministerial Priesthood, *Inter Insigniores*, October 15, 1976. See also John Paul II, apostolic letter *Mulieris Dignitatem*, August 15, 1988, no. 26.

Gospels at home; but only in the House of God—and nowhere else—can you hear and see the Consecration of the body and blood of the Lord." [2]

St. John tells us what happened in the Upper Room after the meal. Our Lord spoke; at first, he was interrupted by three of his apostles, but after that his hearers did not think of questioning him anymore. The Savior's discourse moved them deeply. Jesus alone spoke, the disciples listened; they would listen to him forever. Before long, Jesus was speaking to them no longer, he was addressing the Father. They all held their breath. Jesus prayed.

Isn't this situation almost exactly like that which is reproduced in the Mass? Only the priest proclaims the Eucharistic Prayer by virtue of his ordination.[3] We have heard the Lord's teaching; we have prayed aloud together, beseeching his mediation. Now the priest speaks *in persona Christi*. All things considered, it would be better that no other human voice should make itself heard: Jesus is going to pray with us and for us.

In this prayer, we announce to the world the death and resurrection of the Lord. This is the paschal message that transforms us interiorly, turning us into heralds of the Good News.

OUR FAITH seems to us too faint and our love too little to allow us to accompany our Lord in his oblation and hymn of praise to the Father. But we believe because it is Jesus Christ who has revealed to us this wonderful mystery. We believe in Christ's word—*nil hoc verbo Veritatis verius* (there is no truer token than Truth's own word), as we sing in that masterpiece of eucharistic hymns, the *Adoro Te Devote* of St. Thomas Aquinas.

---

2 *Sermon*, 281.

3 "It is reserved to the priest, by virtue of his ordination, to proclaim the Eucharistic Prayer, which of its nature is the high point of the whole celebration. It is therefore an abuse to have some parts of the Eucharistic Prayer said by the deacon, by a lower minister, or by the faithful. On the other hand the assembly does not remain passive and inert: it unites itself to the priest in faith and silence and shows its concurrence by the various interventions provided for in the course of the Eucharistic Prayer: the responses to the Preface dialogue, the Sanctus, the acclamation after the Consecration, and the final Amen after the *Per Ipsum* [Through him . . .]. The *Per Ipsum* itself is reserved to the priest. This Amen especially should be emphasized by being sung, since it is the most important in the whole Mass" (ID, no. 4).

St. John Chrysostom had these most fitting words to offer on one occasion when he was instructing his faithful about the eucharistic mystery:

> Let us submit to God in all things and not contradict him, even if what he says seems to contradict our reason and intellect; let his words prevail over our reason and intellect. Let us act in this way with regard to the eucharistic mysteries, and not limit our attention just to what can be perceived by the senses, but instead hold fast to his words. For his word cannot deceive.[4]

We believe and we want to love; we do not want to be like the disciples who fell asleep in the supreme moment when Jesus prepared himself for the holocaust. "I believe, Lord, but help my unbelief!" (Mk 9:24), we should say with that man, the father of the boy who was possessed by the devil. "Lord, you know everything; you know I love you" (Jn 21:17), we should repeat once and again. In that way, we can go beyond the limited horizons of our egoism—as a person in love strives to overcome his personal limitations and sings when he wants to serenade his beloved. As Christ offers himself to the Father, we must join him, as a living part of the Church, his Mystical Body. What a pity if we allow Christ to go on without us, if we spurn him.

Therefore, we should "be awake and praying" (Mt 26:41), following Christ from the Upper Room to the cross, to realize "how little a life is to offer to God." [5] Thus, we will finally shed our nasty habit of bargaining with God.

The elements of the Eucharistic Prayer

The chief elements of the Eucharistic Prayer are:

> *Thanksgiving* (expressed especially in the Preface): In the name of the entire people of God, the priest praises the Father and

---

4 *Homily on Matthew*, 82.4: PG 58:743.
5 J. Escrivá de Balaguer, *The Way*, no. 420.

gives thanks to him for the whole work of salvation or for some special aspect of it that corresponds to the day, feast, or season.

Acclamation: Joining with the angels, the congregation sings or recites the *Sanctus*. This acclamation is an intrinsic part of the Eucharistic Prayer, and all the people join with the priest in singing or reciting it.

Epiclesis (invocation): In special invocations, the Church calls on God's power and asks that gifts offered by human hands be consecrated, that they become Christ's body and blood, and that the Victim to be received in Communion be the source of salvation for those who will partake of it.

Narrative of the Institution and Consecration: In the words and actions of Christ, that sacrifice is celebrated which he himself instituted at the Last Supper, when he offered, under the appearances of bread and wine, his body and blood, gave them to his apostles to eat and drink, and then commanded that they reenact this mystery.

Anamnesis (memorial): In fulfillment of the command received from Christ through the apostles, the Church keeps his memorial by recalling especially his passion, resurrection, and ascension.

Oblation: The oblation or offering of the victim is part of a sacrifice. In this memorial, the Church, and in particular the Church here and now assembled, offers the spotless Victim to the Father in the Holy Spirit. The Church's intention is that the faithful not only offer the Victim but also learn to offer themselves and so to surrender themselves, through Christ the Mediator, to an ever more complete union with the Father and with each other, so that at last God may be all in all.

Intercessions: The intercessions make it clear that the Eucharist is celebrated in communion with the entire Church and all its members, living and dead, who are called to share in the salvation and redemption purchased by Christ's body and blood.

This part includes also the commemoration of the saints in whose glory we hope to share.

Final Doxology: The praise of God is expressed in the doxology, to which the people's acclamation is an assent and a conclusion.

The Eucharistic Prayer calls for all not only to listen in silent reverence, but also to take part through the acclamations for which the rite makes provision.[6]

Variety of Eucharistic Prayers

In the Roman rite, the first part of the Eucharistic Prayer, known as the Preface, has acquired many different texts in the course of the centuries. There were twenty Prefaces in the missal at the time of Pope John XXIII.

The second part, known as the Canon, assumed an unchanging form. By contrast, the Oriental liturgies have admitted a certain variety in their Anaphoras. After the Second Vatican Council, Pope Paul VI added three more Eucharistic Prayers, keeping the very venerable Roman Canon.

The Roman Canon is called "Roman" because it originated in Rome at the end of the fourth century. It developed its present form during the pontificate of Gregory the Great in the seventh century and has had no significant changes since then.

It consists of fifteen prayers often described as "tiles in a mosaic." We may look at all fifteen and see their total effect, or we may go line by line and enjoy each prayer.

This Eucharistic Prayer may be used any day. It is particularly fitting on days when there are special texts for the prayers *In union with the whole Church* . . . and the prayer *Father, accept this offering*. . . .

The Second Eucharistic Prayer is the most ancient Anaphora. It follows closely the *Anaphora of Saint Hippolytus*, written at about the year 215. It is vigorous and clear, and has a solid biblical and theological background. Its features make it particularly suitable for week-

---

[6] GIRM, no. 55.

days. Although it has its Preface, it may also be used with other Prefaces.

The Third Eucharistic Prayer is rich with overtones of ancient Alexandrian, Byzantine, and Maronite Anaphoras. It expresses the doctrine of the Eucharist as the sacrifice of Christ in an especially clear way. It gives prominence to the Holy Spirit, naming him four times. Its use is particularly suited to Sundays and holy days. It may be said with any Preface.

The Fourth Eucharistic Prayer provides a fuller summary of the history of salvation. It borrows some elements from the Eastern liturgies, and even from the liturgy of the synagogue. It is a profoundly biblical prayer which recounts the main events in the history of salvation and links this history to its center: Christ. This Eucharistic Prayer has a fixed Preface; therefore, it cannot be used when a Mass has its own proper Preface.[7]

There are other Eucharistic Prayers for especial occasions: three Eucharistic Prayers for Masses of children, two for Masses of reconciliation, and the so-called Eucharistic Prayer of the Swiss Synod for Masses with some ecclesial character.

[7] GIRM, no. 322d. A Preface is considered "proper" in a strict sense when it is attached to Masses celebrated on the very day of the feast or during its *octave*. There are Prefaces indicated for entire Seasons of the year, but these are not to be regarded as "proper" in a strict sense: *Notitiae* 5 (1969) 323, n. 1.

22. The Preface

Let us stretch out our hearts and hands to God in heaven
(Lam 3:41).

The Preface is the beginning of the Eucharistic Prayer. During the early years of Christianity, the term *preface* indicated some solemn prayer of thanksgiving proffered before a congregation.[1] Hence, it referred to the entire Eucharistic Prayer. Later on, it referred only to the introduction, and this varied according to the feast celebrated. The rest of the Eucharistic Prayer, called the *Canon*, became fixed in form.

The Preface is basically an act of thanksgiving in a literary form between prayer and hymn. It seeks to move the faithful to praise and joy. In order to be easily understood, it is rather brief, but substantial in content.

Once the Prayer over the Gifts is said, the priest addresses himself to us with hands extended and greets us in the usual manner, "The Lord be with you." We answer, "And also with you."

Then he invites us to set our thoughts on God alone. He stands with uplifted hands as though he would bear aloft our most pressing desires and expectations. With one voice, we raise our hearts to acclaim the Lord. The priest exhorts us, "Lift up your hearts." We answer, "We lift them up to the Lord." This response befits us as members of the Mystical Body of Christ, for our Head is in heaven.

A fraternal sharing of personal decisions and aspirations is thus established—as if each one felt the need to be strengthened by everybody else's optimism and daring to climb the mountain, as Moses did, and meet God. The priest continues, and urges us on: "Let us give thanks to the Lord, our God." And we answer, "It is right to give him thanks and praise." Not one word of this dialogue has changed since the third century. Almost without realizing it, we find

---

[1] The word *praefatio* with this meaning was already known to followers of the old pagan cult. They said: *praefari divos* (Virgil), *praefari Vestam* (Ovid). Here the preposition *prae-* indicates something done in front of someone, and not before something else.

ourselves affirming that it is right to give thanks to God always and everywhere, through Jesus Christ, our Lord.

> Our Lord began the Last Supper giving thanks. Penitence, confidence in God, adoration, all these things too, of course, are perfectly in place for us, but the characteristic attitude of the Christian people in worshiping God is thankfulness. That is why we call it the Holy Eucharist. First and foremost, the Mass means reminding ourselves of our redemption—Jesus Christ was crucified for me. First and foremost, then, we are catching our breath at a great deliverance, and thanking God for it. 2

An offering in the form of thanksgiving was a mode of prayer frequently used by the Christians of the early centuries, as they had grown accustomed to it in the Eucharist.3 This fundamental attitude of gratefulness to God is evident, for instance, in the letters of St. Paul, which almost always begin with an act of thanksgiving. In turn, the spirit of thanksgiving for the coming of the Lord, for his passion and death, and for his resurrection and ascension gave shape to the Prefaces of the Roman liturgy. "Thank you . . . ," we repeat, echoing the priest's words, so that the delicate flower of gratefulness may really bloom in our hearts.

> We thank you for all that is beautiful in the world and for the happiness you have given us. We praise you for daylight and for your word which lights up our minds. We praise you for the earth and all the people who live in it and for our life which comes from you. 4

We thank God for our being children of such a loving and provident Father. Once again in the Mass, we show our appreciation to God,

2 See R. Knox, *The Mass in Slow Motion* (New York: Sheed & Ward, 1948), p. 89.

3 "Notice, for example, the last prayer of St. Polycarp, who was martyred in the year 155. . . . Condemned to be burned alive, [he] climbed the pyre, and whilst being tied to the stake he lifted up his eyes to Heaven and prayed: 'O Lord, God Almighty, . . . I bless thee that this day, at this very hour, thou has found me worthy to drink the chalice of thy Christ. . . . I praise thee, I bless thee, I glorify thee, through the eternal and heavenly High Priest, Jesus Christ' " (G. Chevrot, *Our Mass*, p. 118).

4 Preface of the Children's Eucharistic Prayer.

whose plan, formed long ago and fulfilled by Christ, opened for us the way of salvation.[5] Although the words, particular aspects, and points of departure vary in each Preface, our attention is always drawn to the figure of Christ and his work of redemption.

Sometimes, the priest says of Christ:

His future coming was proclaimed by all the prophets.
The Virgin Mother bore him in her womb with love beyond all telling.
John the Baptist was his herald
and made him known when at last he came.[6]

At other times, we are reminded that:

He freed us from sin and death
and called us to the glory that has made us
a chosen race, a royal priesthood,
a holy nation, a people set apart.[7]

The first Preface of the Eucharist makes a reference to Christ as:

The true and eternal priest
who established this unending sacrifice.
He offered himself as a victim for our deliverance
and taught us to make this offering in his memory.

And in another Preface, the priest says:

Though his nature was divine,
he stripped himself of glory
and by shedding his blood on the cross
he brought his peace to the world.
Therefore he was exalted above all creation
and became the source of eternal life
to all who serve him.[8]

Through Christ, we now move up to the Father:

Father in heaven, . . .
Through all eternity you live in unapproachable light.

[5] Preface of Advent I.
[6] Preface of Advent II.
[7] Preface of Sundays in Ordinary Time I.
[8] Weekdays Preface I.

Source of life and goodness, you have created all things,
to fill your creatures with every blessing
and lead all men to the joyful vision of your light.[9]

We conclude the Preface by joining the choirs of angels in their majestic hymn of praise for the Three Divine Persons: the *Sanctus*.

How beautiful is the Communion of the Saints! We join our own voices with those of the hosts of angels in awe, wonderment, and great enthusiasm.

The angels are pure spiritual creatures of God. Jesus Christ "has made the angels and Dominations and Powers his subjects" (1 Pet 3:22), because he, "as Head, would bring everything together under him, everything in the heavens and everything on earth" (Eph 1:10).[10]

St. John Chrysostom describes the presence of the angels during the Holy Sacrifice of the Mass with these words:

The angels surround the priest; all the temple, especially the sanctuary, is populated with celestial hosts of angels who honor God, present on the altar.[11]

St. Thomas Aquinas also affirms:

It is believed that the angels visit the assemblies of the faithful, especially when the holy mysteries are celebrated.[12]

And Blessed Josemaría Escrivá points out that aside from the angels, our Blessed Mother is somehow present during the Mass, and joins us in praise of God:

I adore and praise with the angels; it is not difficult, because I know that, as I celebrate the holy Mass, they surround me, adoring the Blessed Trinity. And I know that in some way

---

[9] Preface of the Eucharistic Prayer IV.
[10] See also Eph 1:21; Col 1:16; Is 6:2; Ez 10:1ff., among others.
[11] *Treatise on Priesthood*, VI, 4.
[12] *Ad I Cor.*, 11:10.

the Blessed Virgin is there, because of her intimate relationship with the most Blessed Trinity and because she is the Mother of Jesus Christ, perfect God and perfect man. . . . In his veins runs the blood of his Mother, the blood that is offered in the sacrifice of redemption, on Calvary and in the Mass.[13]

---

[13] J. Escrivá de Balaguer, *Christ Is Passing By*, no. 89.

23. *The* Sanctus: *An Acclamation of the Triune God*

I saw the Lord Yahweh seated on a high throne; his train filled the
sanctuary; and above him stood seraphs. . . . And they cried out
one to another in this way, "Holy, holy, holy is Yahweh Sabaoth.
His glory fills the whole earth" (Is 6:1–3).

The Eucharistic Prayer is reserved for the priest. However, this solemn prayer that began with the Preface is now interrupted to allow
us to intervene with the *Sanctus*. We sing with the entire creation
that mysterious passage in Isaiah 6:1–3, wherein the prophet tells us
of his vision of God. The seraphim were gathered around the throne,
extolling the thrice-holy Lord of all creation, when God revealed his
mission to the prophet. We add to this acclamation, the psalms and
hosannas that resounded in Jerusalem on Psalm Sunday.[1]

Holy, holy, holy Lord, God of power and might,
heaven and earth are full of your glory.
Hosanna in the highest.
Blessed is he who comes in the name of the Lord.
Hosanna in the highest.

Cardinal Bona (seventeenth century) explains that this hymn contains three praises and two petitions:

First, we extol the holiness, power, and supreme dominion
of God, when we say, "Holy, holy, holy Lord, God of
power and might."
Then, we praise his glory which shines forth in all creatures, when we say, "Heaven and earth are full of your
glory."
Third, we laud Christ by saying, "Blessed is he who
comes in the name of the Lord." While saying this, we
invite him to come to our souls with the same affection and

[1] Mt 29:9; Mk 11:9; Ps 118:26.

devotion with which his Blessed Mother received him at
the annunciation.

The two petitions are: "Hosanna in the highest"; we say
it twice, asking for our salvation and everything that leads to
it. The first petition is addressed to God, and the second to
Christ.

The same author adds: "This hymn is placed at the beginning of the
Eucharistic Prayer so that we realize we are involved in a very important business. We are before the throne of his Divine Majesty, entering the Holy of Holies. If until now it was convenient for us to be
pure and devout, henceforward we should be inflamed with so much
love that we might set fire to all present; even more, to the whole
world." [2]

This hymn does not appear in the ancient liturgy. Its inclusion in
the Mass is attributed to Pope St. Sixtus I (119–128). Among the
Greeks, the hymn is called the *Trisagion*.

Now, let us consider him who triumphed. After the *hosannas* were
silent, Jesus shed tears over Jerusalem. He wept over the lot of those
people who were to reject the cross and repudiate their vocation. His
disciples did not understand, either, the nature of his unending rule.
A few branches torn from palms still lay in the streets and were not
yet withered when the King is raised up, nailed to the murderers'
cross. "Scandal and madness," some say; for us the mystery of the
cross is "the power and wisdom of God" (1 Cor 1:24).

Is it not true that as soon as you cease to be afraid of the
cross, of what people call the cross, when you set your will
to accept the will of God, then you find happiness, and all
your worries, all your sufferings, physical or moral, pass
away?

Truly the cross of Jesus is gentle and lovable. There, sorrows cease to count; there is only the joy of knowing that
we are co-redeemers with him. [3]

[2] J. Cardinal Bona, *De Sacrif. Missae.*
[3] J. Escrivá de Balaguer, *The Way of the Cross*, Second Station.

24. The Epiclesis: Invocation to the Holy Spirit

For if the blood of goats and bulls and the sprinkled ashes of a heifer sanctify the unclean unto the cleansing of the flesh, how much more will the blood of Christ, who through the Holy Spirit offered himself unblemished unto God, cleanse your conscience from dead works to serve the living God? (Heb 9:13–14).

In the Epiclesis, the priest requests God the Father to send the Holy Spirit so that the bread and wine offered may become Christ's body and blood and so we may be able to celebrate the eucharistic mystery, and to make all the effects of the sacrament operative in us.

At the same time, the priest extends his hands, palms downward,[1] over the chalice and host, and traces the sign of the cross over them. With this gesture, he asks God to pour his blessing over the gifts offered and to turn them into his Son's body and blood.

St. Thomas Aquinas asks himself, "Why does the priest ask for what he positively knows will happen at the Consecration?" And he answers, "How many times did Jesus Christ ask for what he well knew would infallibly happen? The priest seems to pray, not so much for the miracle of transubstantiation as for the happy fruits it may produce in our souls."

After the last notes of the *Sanctus*, the people again fall silent. For it is how man should approach God—in silence.

In the Old Testament, the high priest, carrying the blood of the victims (Heb 9:7), entered alone the Holy of Holies once a year. Leaving behind the people, he offered a sacrifice to God in an atmosphere of awe and respect for God.

In the early Middle Ages, the priest entered the sanctuary, and curtains were drawn, thus isolating him from the people. To accentuate the importance of this part of the Mass, clerics carrying candles

---

[1] It is inspired by the Mosaic ritual (Lev 1:4; Ex 29:10). The high priest placed both his hands on the head of the scapegoat, thus symbolically heaping upon it the sins of the Israelites (Lev 16:21).

placed themselves on either side of the altar. This is the origin of the custom of placing a lighted candle on the altar during the Eucharistic Prayer. The people attended these ceremonies kneeling.

In the Roman Canon, the Epiclesis begins with:

We come to you, Father,
with praise and thanksgiving,
through Jesus Christ your Son.
Through him we ask you to accept and bless ✠
these gifts we offer you in sacrifice.

The original Latin version of the First Eucharistic Prayer acknowledges God the Father as *clementissime Pater* (our most loving and merciful Father) so that we may deal with him with the confidence of children.

At this point, the Epiclesis is interrupted with a first series of intercessions. (There are two such series.) The invocation is resumed with greater intensity and expressed with greater detail afterward. With hands outstretched over the offerings, the priest says,

Bless and approve our offering; make it acceptable to you,
an offering in spirit and in truth.
Let it become for us the body and blood of Jesus Christ,
your only Son, our Lord.

If we read these two parts in sequence, we will recognize the original idea in them, that of intercession. These parts are to be found in the very oldest forms of the Roman Canon.

In the original Latin, the Son of God is referred to as *dilectissimi Filii tui* (your most beloved Son). His work of salvation is now getting close to completion, and the Church shows her appreciation with delicate expressions of tenderness.

We find the Epiclesis at the beginning of the Second and Third Eucharistic Prayers. On the other hand, the Fourth Eucharistic Prayer, which has its own Preface, links it, after the *Sanctus*, with a narrative of the history of salvation in the form of *anamnesis* (remembrance). The Epiclesis comes after:

Father, may this Holy Spirit sanctify these offerings.
Let them become the body ✠ *and blood of Jesus Christ our Lord*

as we celebrate the great mystery which he left us
as an everlasting covenant.

How often have we relegated the Holy Spirit to a secondary role. We now promise him we shall be more docile to his sanctifying action. "That means we should be aware of the work of the Holy Spirit all around us, and in our own selves we should recognize the gifts he distributes, the movements and institutions he inspires, the affections and decisions he provokes in our hearts." [2]

---

[2] J. Escrivá de Balaguer, *Christ Is Passing By*, no. 130.

25. In the Quiet of the Upper Room

On the same night that he was betrayed, the Lord Jesus took some bread, and thanked God for it and broke it, and he said, "This is my body, which is for you; do this as a memorial of me." In the same way he took the cup after supper, and said, "This cup is the new covenant in my blood. Whenever you drink it, do this as a memorial of me" (1 Cor 11:23–25).

The Institution Narrative and Consecration

What mankind has been waiting for through centuries is now going to take place among us. God has arranged everything to happen at its own time and in the most fitting manner. At this moment, we are invited to a greater recollection and devotion. To remind us about this, a little before the Consecration, the server may ring a bell as a signal to the faithful. Depending on local custom, he also rings the bell at the elevation of both the host and the chalice.[1]

The priest pronounces the words of the Consecration.

FOR THE BREAD:
Take this, all of you, and eat it:
this is my body which will be given up for you.

FOR THE WINE:
Take this all of you, and drink from it:
this is the cup of my blood,
the blood of the new and everlasting covenant.
It will be shed for you and for all men
so that sins may be forgiven.
Do this in memory of me.

The Consecration is the essential part of the Mass. The human minister has received, with his ordination, the power to pro-

---

[1] GIRM, no. 109.

nounce the great and wonderful prayers of the Consecration; and these will be effective. In truth, he is but the instrument of Christ. "The priest offers the Holy Sacrifice *in persona Christi*; this means more than offering 'in the name of' or 'in the place of' Christ. *In persona* means in specific sacramental identification with 'the Eternal High Priest' who is the author and principal subject of this sacrifice of his, a sacrifice in which, in truth, nobody can take his place." [2]

The priest does not act on his own account. "The priest's identity consists in being a direct and daily instrument of the saving grace which Christ has won for us." That is why, "if you ever come across a priest who, apparently, does not seem to live in keeping with the Gospel, do not judge him; let God judge him. Bear also in mind that if he celebrates Mass validly, with the intention of consecrating, our Lord would still come down into his hands however unworthy they are." [3]

The priest's own personality is blotted out in order to clothe himself with the person of the everlasting Priest. It is Jesus Christ himself who, at every Mass, performs the Consecration, while the priest lends him his voice. The priest repeats the words pronounced by Christ, not as he would describe the history of some beautiful event that happened in the past, but as bearing the same effective power Christ attached to them.

After the Consecration, what were bread and wine are no longer bread and wine, although our senses continue to perceive them as such, with all their sensible attributes. But it is now Christ himself—with his body, blood, soul, and divinity—who is there, under the appearances of bread and wine, offering himself to the Father for the redemption of all.

The full work of our redemption is truly and effectively carried out in the Mass, not only in a symbolic manner. "To accomplish so great a work [the work of redemption], Christ is always present in his Church, especially in her liturgical celebrations; he is present in the sacrifice of the Mass, not only in the person of his minister, 'the same one now offering, through the ministry of the priests, who formerly

---

[2] DC, no. 8. See also *S. Th.*, III, q. 82, a. 7; LG, no. 10; PO, 2.
[3] J. Escrivá de Balaguer, *A Priest Forever*, pp. 8–9.

offered himself on the cross,' [4] but especially under the eucharistic species." [5]

This is the same body that was hanging on the cross, the same blood that was poured there: We should repeat these truths once and again until we truly believe them and begin really to love. Before the eucharistic mystery, it is necessary for us, more than ever, to be humble. We need to acknowledge the existence of a wall: our own insufficiency to understand fully the unfathomable reality that the Eucharist contains. We firmly believe that reality because of the word of God, and our whole faith is brought into play when we believe in Jesus, really present in the sacrament.

Human reasoning must give way to faith; now, we can repeat to ourselves the oath that Pope St. Gregory VII commanded Berengarius to swear:

> I believe in my heart and openly profess that the bread and wine, which are placed on the altar, through the mystery of the sacred prayer and the words of the Redeemer are substantially changed into the true and proper and life-giving flesh and blood of Jesus Christ our Lord. After the Consecration it is the true body of Christ, which was born of the Virgin, and which hung on the cross as an offering for the salvation of the world, and which sits at the right hand of the Father. And the true blood of Christ which flowed from his side. And Christ is present not just as a sign and by reason of the power of the sacrament, but in his proper nature and true substance. This I believe.[6]

Referring to the consecrated species, St. Cyril of Jerusalem (314–386) teaches: "Do not think these are just plain bread and plain wine. They are the body and blood of Christ, as the Lord asserted. Faith must convince you of the latter even though your senses suggest you the former. Do not judge about this according to your preferences but, based on your faith, believe with firmness and cer-

---

[4] SC, no. 7; Council of Trent, *Doctrine of the Sacrifice of the Mass*, ch. 2.
[5] J. Escrivá de Balaguer, *A Priest Forever*, pp. 7–8.
[6] Mansi, *Collectio amplissima Conciliorum*, 20:524D.

tainty that you have been made worthy of the body and blood of Christ." [7]

St. Ambrose (339–397) also is explicit:

> Perhaps you say, The bread which I brought is ordinary bread.—Yes, it is ordinary bread before the sacramental words; but as soon as the Consecration takes place, that bread becomes Christ's flesh. Let us continue. How can that which is bread be the body of Christ?—By Consecration. Of what words is Consecration made up, and whose words are they?—Those of the Lord Jesus. For all the rest that has been said previously is said by the priest: the praises of God, prayers for the people, for the rulers, for all others. But as soon as the moment at which the venerable sacrament comes into being is reached, the priest no longer speaks of himself, but uses the words of Christ. It is thus Christ's word which makes this sacrament.
>
> The Lord commanded so and heavens were made, the Lord commanded so and the earth was made. He commanded so and the seas were made, the Lord commanded so and all creatures came into existence. Behold, what power the word of Christ has. And if the word of the Lord Jesus has so much power to create things out of nothing, surely, it must be effective to turn existing things into something else. Therefore, listen, I want you to be absolutely sure of this teaching: It was not the body of Christ before the Consecration, but I tell you, after the Consecration it is the body of Christ. He said it, and it was made; he commanded so and it was created. [8]

Encouraged by the words of these Fathers of the early Church, we should not worry if our faith is not accompanied by lofty or pious feelings, if we are not gripped by tender emotions, during the Mass. The real test for our faith and love for the Eucharist comes after the Mass, during the day: in our faithful dedication to our ordinary

---

[7] *Catechesis Mystagogical*, IV.

[8] This is thought to be an edition of notes taken by a listener to his doctrinal lectures: *De Sacramentis*, IV, 15.

work, in our generous service to all and each of our brothers, in the delicate fulfillment of our practices of piety. Now, in the Mass, it is enough to have strong desires of believing, loving, and rectifying, of promising, of asking. Let us express all these desires with a "My Lord and my God!" as St. Thomas did. It will speak simply but also most eloquently of our self-surrender, of our sorrow, of our conversion, and of our decision to follow him, when the Lord comes down upon the altar as the priest utters the words of the Consecration.

Adoration of the Word Incarnate

At the elevation the priest shows us the consecrated host and the chalice and genuflects each time.[9] It is said that this ceremony was instituted as a protest against the errors of Berengarius of Tours (eleventh century) concerning Christ's presence in the Eucharist. We know that Bishop Eudes de Sully (who died in 1208) prescribed the elevation in his diocese of Paris; soon after that, it gained acceptance at Rome.

Three things are intended by the elevation of the sacred host:

To expose Jesus Christ, now present on the altar, to the adoration of the faithful.

To re-present the elevation of Jesus Christ's body on the cross. He said, "And I, when I am lifted up from the earth, will draw all things to myself" (Jn 12:32). This is the mystery of Christ that we commemorate: his incarnation, his life of work in Nazareth, his preaching and miracles, his death and resurrection. Through this great mystery, Christ is the center of the universe, the firstborn and Lord of all creation. "St. Paul gave a motto to the Christians at Ephesus: Instaurare omnia in Christo (Eph 1:10): to fill everything with the spirit of Jesus, placing Christ at the center of everything." [10] This should also be the program of our life.

---

[9] The genuflection is a gesture of adoration. It ought to be calm, serene, and reverent, and certainly not a bob done by leaning on the altar.

[10] J. Escrivá de Balaguer, Christ Is Passing By, no. 105.

To offer to God in silence this only one Victim of our salvation, as the priests of the Old Testament offered God their lambs as victims by elevating them.[11]

During the elevation, we should glance at the eucharistic species in adoration. But we should also remember that we have come to Mass not only to worship Jesus Christ present in the sacrament of the altar. That could be done equally well in the Exposition of and Benediction with the Blessed Sacrament. We come to Mass also to offer Jesus Christ on the cross with the priest and the entire Church, and to offer ourselves to God with Jesus Christ and as part of his Mystical Body. In other words, we come mainly to share in the sacrifice of Jesus Christ. As part of the Church, we are united to Christ in the act wherein he himself offers his sacrifice to his Father.

The Acclamation

Since the seventh century, the expression *mysterium fidei* (now rendered, "Let us proclaim the mystery of faith") has appeared united to the consecratory formula. At first, it was within the formula itself; now, it is at the end. But it is unmistakably an invitation for us to respond. We have four responses commonly used in English:

> *Christ has died, Christ is risen, Christ will come again.*

> *Lord, by your cross and resurrection you have set us free. You are the Savior of the world.*

> *Dying you destroyed our death, rising you restored our life. Lord Jesus, come in glory.*

> *When we eat this bread and drink this cup, we proclaim your death, Lord Jesus, until you come in glory.*

When we recite any of these acclamations, we in effect declare and give witness to the encounter of the risen Christ and Mary Magdalene on Easter Sunday. Like her, we should join our life with the Life

---

[11] See P. Chaignon, *The Sacrifice of the Mass* (New York: Benzinger, 1951), pp. 143–144.

which is offered on Calvary. For Christ is the way; in him we find everything. Outside him our life is empty.

We will find the meaning of our life by sharing the Victim's offering and by proclaiming the message of the cross and resurrection among our peers, announcing it through what we say and do.

> Men have not been created just to build the best possible world. We have been put here on earth for a further purpose: to enter into communion with God himself. Jesus has promised us not a life of ease or worldly achievement, but the house of his Father God, which awaits us at the end of the way.
>
> The Lord wants Christians to live in such a way that the people we deal with will find in our conduct—despite our weaknesses, faults and failings—an echo of the drama of love that was Calvary. Everything we have comes from God; he wants us to be salt which flavors and light which brings the happy news that he is a Father who loves without measure. The Christian is the salt and light of the world, not because he conquers or triumphs, but because he bears witness to God's love. And he won't be salt if he can't give flavor. Nor will he be light if he doesn't bear witness to Jesus through his example and word, if he loses sight of the purpose of his life.[12]

12 J. Escrivá de Balaguer, *Christ Is Passing By*, no. 100.

26. The Anamnesis: Memorial of Christ's Passion and Death

Until the Lord comes, therefore, every time you eat this bread and drink this cup, you are proclaiming his death (1 Cor 11:26).

The Anamnesis is a prayer of remembrance in which the Church calls to mind the Lord's passion, resurrection, and ascension into heaven.

This part of the Canon, called *Anamnesis* (memorial), comes after the acclamation of the Consecration. We have just been asked to "proclaim the mystery of faith." And what is this mystery? Precisely the redeeming sacrifice of Christ celebrated in these rites. We are now reminded that the Church is acting in memory of our Lord and obeying his explicit command: "Do this in memory of me." We are mindful of Christ's mandate, and nothing is more moving than this assertion of fidelity to Christ's express indication. It is against this background that the Church declares that the Eucharist is a *sacramental reenactment* of Christ's death on Calvary and not an attempt to "add to" the sacrifice on the cross.

The Roman Canon mentions our share in Christ's sacrifice explicitly:

> *We, your [holy] people and your ministers, . . .*
> *offer to you, God of glory and majesty,*
> *this holy and perfect sacrifice.*[1]

In other words, we are not mere spectators; rather, we play an active part: *we offer*. But we should make a distinction here. The *common priesthood* of all baptized persons empowers us to offer the Mass. On the other hand, the priest, having received the sacrament of Holy Orders, possesses the *ministerial priesthood* that empowers him to *celebrate* the Mass.

Lay people are members of the *laos*, the people of God, which is "holy." The epistle of St. Peter provides us the frame of mind to

---

[1] "*Nos servi tui sed et plebs tua sancta . . . offerimus praeclarae maiestati tuae . . .*"

recall the passion, death, and resurrection of Christ.[2] United to the entire Church, as well as to our brothers who have been faithful to their Christian vocation, we now offer Christ's sacrifice with the desire that it become the center of our daily life and apostolic eagerness. Meanwhile, "the Church presses forward amid persecutions of the world and the consolations of God, announcing the cross and death of the Lord until he comes." [3]

We not only announce what happened in the past but also prophesy what is to come: the final fulfillment of the kingdom, the light which knows no setting.

THE Anamnesis of the Second Eucharistic Prayer is both vigorous and clear:

> *In memory of his death and resurrection,*
> *we offer you, Father, this life-giving bread,*
> *this saving cup.*
> *We thank you for counting us worthy*
> *to stand in your presence and serve you.*

It takes us back to the times of the martyrs; it reproduces the text of the *Anaphora of St. Hippolytus* (dating from about A.D. 215) with almost no variations:

> *Remembering, therefore, his death and resurrection,*
> *we offer to you the bread and the cup,*
> *giving thanks to you, because of*
> *your having accounted us as worthy*
> *to stand before you and minister to you.*

In the Third and Fourth Eucharistic Prayers, we find the following characteristics:

The *expectation* of the coming of the Lord is explicitly stated.

The *sacrificial character* of the Eucharist is stressed, showing that Christ is the direct object of the offering.

---

[2] "You are a chosen race, a royal priesthood, a consecrated nation, a people set apart to sing the praises of God who called you out of the darkness into his wonderful light" (1 Pet 2:9).

[3] LG, no. 8.

An *element of thanksgiving* has been added to that of memorial.

This is the Anamnesis of the Fourth Eucharistic Prayer:

Father, we now celebrate this memorial of our redemption.
We recall Christ's death, his descent among the dead,
his resurrection, and his ascension to your right hand;
and, looking forward to his coming in glory,
we offer you his body and blood,
the acceptable sacrifice
which brings salvation to the whole world.

FOLLOWING the footprints of Jesus, our life becomes a *prolonged Mass.* Here is a summary or program of life by which we can achieve this ideal:

- To remember Christ's passion and death. It delivered us from the *real evil—sin*; and merited for us all true good.

- To experience constantly the *joy* of his resurrection.

- To *proclaim* his resurrection and ascension, through our words and deeds.

- To *center our day* on this holy sacrifice, while we look forward to Christ's coming.

27. The Oblation

Try, then, to imitate God, as children of his that he loves, and fol-low Christ . . . giving himself up in our place as a fragrant offer-ing and a sacrifice to God (Eph 51–52).

In the Offertory, the priest asked the Lord to accept the bread and wine as a token of the gift of our persons. Now, the Consecration has taken place, and the bread and wine are no longer there; they have been changed into the body and blood of Jesus Christ. This Christ we offer to God.

In this memorial, the Church—and in particular we, here and now assembled—offers the spotless Victim to the Father in the Holy Spirit.[1] The Church, through the priest, addresses herself to God the Father,

Lord, look upon this sacrifice which you have given to your Church;
and by your Holy Spirit, gather all who share this one bread and one cup
into the one body of Christ, a living sacrifice of praise.[2]

The Roman Canon formulates the oblation or offering with words that echo the biblical sacrifices:

Look with favor on these offerings
and accept them as once you accepted
the gifts of your servant Abel,
the sacrifice of Abraham, our father in faith,
and the bread and wine offered by your priest Melchisedech.

Bowing, with hands joined, the priest continues:

Almighty God,
we pray that your angel may take this sacrifice
to your altar in heaven.

---

[1] GIRM, no. 55f.
[2] Eucharistic Prayer IV.

Then, as we receive from this altar
the sacred body and blood of your Son, . . .

He stands up straight and makes the sign of the cross, continuing,

let us be filled with every grace and blessing.

WE READ in the Bible how Abel the Just offered God "the firstborn of his flock" and how "God looked with favor on Abel and his offering" (Gen 4:4). Abel's offering came from a clean and sincere heart. Unfortunately, his brother Cain could not stand his attitude and therefore slew him. Our thoughts go to Jesus, the real Just Man, put to death on the cross by his brothers out of hatred.

God was also well pleased with the sacrifice offered by Melchisedech, king of Jerusalem. He made a sudden and mysterious appearance to offer bread and wine to God Most High and to bless Abraham (Gen 14:17–20). The Church has always recognized in this sacrifice a figure of Christ's sacrifice (see Heb 7).

We ask God to look favorably on this sacrifice and to accept it as he did the sacrifice of the patriarchs mentioned in the Roman Canon. But we actually offer much more than Melchisedech's symbolic offerings to God. Ours is a holy sacrifice, the purest of all victims, and one of much greater value. God will accept it because it is Christ's.

While we participate in the Mass, we think of a third sacrifice: that of Abraham. It was the most difficult and painful (Gen 22:1–19). "Take your son," God told Abraham, "your only child Isaac, whom you love, and go to the land of Moriah. There you shall offer him as a burnt offering." Rising early in the morning, Abraham loaded his donkey with the firewood to be used for the burnt offering and took with him two of his servants and his son, Isaac. Upon reaching the place, Abraham took the wood, loaded it on Isaac, and carried in his own hands the fire and the knife. Then the two of them set out together. Isaac spoke to Abraham, "Father, here are the fire and the wood, but where is the lamb for the burnt offering?" Abraham answered, "My son, God himself will provide the lamb."

When they arrived at the place God had pointed out to him, Abraham built an altar there and arranged the wood. Then he bound Isaac and put him on the altar on top of the wood. Abraham stretched out his hand and seized his knife to kill his son. But the angel of the Lord called him from heaven, "Abraham, do not harm the boy. God knows you have not refused your son, your only son." Then, looking up, Abraham saw a ram caught by its horns in a bush. He took it and offered it in place of his son.

God's command was a severe test of Abraham's obedience and also of his faith. Abraham was justified and blessed by God. Another day, a different son, the Son of God no less, will offer himself on the cross, and he will not be spared. From his death we all receive life everlasting as we join his oblation.

However, a note of doubt comes when we focus on the human side of our personal offering which is added to Christ's and is incorporated into it. The Victim offered is infinitely holy, but what about the hands that proffer it? We will be more or less pleasing to God, depending on whether we are saints or mediocrities. It is by our correspondence to his grace through personal struggle that we humbly attract God's merciful gaze. We ask him to give us his grace to foster in ourselves those dispositions which he wants to find in each of us.

Notice the priest's attitude. He bows low, for his petition is bold. The same petition is repeated at the end of the oblation, for the efficacy of Christ's sacrifice on our own souls depends on our dispositions and perseverance. In this prayer, God's adoration on earth is united to that in heaven. It is a reminder that what we celebrate here in signs will find its fulfillment in heaven, our true homeland. We ask God to receive our sacrifice and to inspire us with fitting sentiments so that our participation through Communion may be fruitful.

In the Second, Third, and Fourth Eucharistic Prayers we ask the help of the Holy Spirit to gather all who share this one bread and one cup, so that we may become one body with Christ, a living sacrifice of praise:

> Look with favor on your Church's offering,
> and see the Victim whose death has reconciled us to yourself.
> Grant that we, who are nourished by his body and blood,
> may be filled with his Holy Spirit,
> and become one body, one spirit in Christ.[3]

[3] Eucharistic Prayer III.

The Church's intention is that the faithful not only offer this Victim but also learn to offer themselves and so to surrender themselves, through Christ the Mediator, to an ever more complete union with the Father and with each other, so that at last God may be all in all.[4]

---

[4] GIRM, no. 55f; see also SC, no. 48.

28. *Intercessions*

Yahweh said to Eliphaz of Teman, "So now find seven bullocks and seven rams, and take them back with you to my servant Job and offer a holocaust for yourselves, while Job, my servant, offers prayers for you. I will listen to him with favor and excuse your folly. . . ." He went away to do as Yahweh had ordered, and Yahweh listened to Job with favor (Job 42:8–9).

The mother of Jesus said to him, "They have no wine." Jesus said, "Woman, why turn to me? My hour has not come yet." His mother said to the servants, "Do whatever he tells you." Jesus said to the servants, "Fill the jars with water" (Jn 2:4–7).

Because Christ's sacrifice is the preeminent and eternal act of intercession, the intercessory prayers that form part of the Eucharistic Prayer are suitably placed at the heart of the Anaphora.

At Mass, we not only pray for ourselves, but also join our prayer to that of our brethren. The Intercessions make it clear that we celebrate the Mass in communion with the entire Church in heaven and on earth; and that we make the offering for the Church and for all her members, living and dead.[1]

We tell God in the Fourth Eucharistic Prayer:

Then, in your kingdom, freed from the corruption of sin and death, we shall sing your glory with every creature through Christ our Lord, through whom you give us everything that is good.

"Foreshadowed by Malachias (1:11), this new oblation of the New Testament has always been offered by the Church, in accordance with the teaching of our Lord and the apostles, 'not only to atone for the sins and punishments and satisfactions of the living faithful and to appeal for their other needs, but also to help those

[1] GIRM, no. 55g.

who have died in Christ but have not yet been completely purified.' " [2]

The Intercessions are usually divided into three sections: for living
Christians, for the dead, and in relation to the saints in heaven.

Intercessions for the living

The first generations of Christians prayed constantly for the whole
Church, following Christ's command of mutual love.

We have a testimony, for instance, in the *Didaché*, written about
A.D. 110: "May your Church be gathered from the ends of the world
in your kingdom, as this bread, scattered on the mountains, became
one." [3]

St. Polycarp, the Bishop martyr of Smyrna in 155, prayed aloud
"for all the Catholic Church spread about over all the earth," [4]
before being delivered up to the stake.

And when St. Fructuosus, the Bishop of Tarragona, was going to
the stake in 259, a certain Christian commended himself to him:
"Father, pray for me." The Bishop answered, "It is fitting that I
should pray for the entire Catholic Church, spread out from east to
west." [5]

St. Cyril, Bishop of Jerusalem (314–386), wrote the following for
those he was instructing in the Christian faith:

> After the spiritual sacrifice, the unbloody act of worship, has
> been completed, we bend over this propitiatory offering and
> beg God to grant peace to all the churches, to give harmony
> to the whole world, to bless our rulers, our soldiers and our
> companions, to aid the sick and afflicted, and in general to
> assist all those who stand in need; we all pray for all these
> intentions, and we offer this Victim for them. [6]

[2] DC, 29; quotation from Council of Trent, *Doctrine on the Holy Sacrifice of the Mass*,
c. 2.

[3] *Didaché*, IX, 4; see also X, 5.

[4] *Martyrium Polycarpi*, c. 8.1; see also 5.1.

[5] G. Villada, *Historia eclesiastica de España*, vol. 1, p. 257.

[6] St. Cyril of Jerusalem, *Catechesis*, 23 [*Mystagogical* 5], 8–18: PG 33:1115.

We find similar expressions of intercession in the Eucharistic Prayers:

> Lord, may this sacrifice,
> which has made our peace with you,
> advance the peace and salvation of all the world.
> Strengthen in faith and love your pilgrim Church on earth; . . .
> Father, hear the prayers of the family you have gathered here before you.
> In mercy and love unite all your children wherever they may be.[7]

We pray for the pope and for the bishop of our diocese. This union with them is necessary because "the Church of God is really present in all legitimate organized local groups of faithful, which, in so far they are united to their pastors . . . are called churches."[8]

Two elements are important here: The community must be *legitimately organized*; and the members of the community are the Church when they are *united with their pastors*. What do these conditions mean? They mean, in the first place, that no one can make himself the Church. A group cannot simply come together, read the New Testament, and say, "Now we are the Church because the Lord is found wherever two or three are gathered in his name."[9] They also mean that, like the Eucharist, the Church cannot be made, but can only be *received* by us. To be legitimate, each Mass presupposes union among the faithful, and of the faithful with their bishop, the pope, and the universal Church. Moreover, that solid union is made stronger with the celebration of the Eucharist and is a consequence of it.[10]

Therefore, we feel united now with the pope's Mass, and with that of our bishop, and pray for both of them by name. In that way, the words of Pope Pelagius (in 561) won't apply to us: "How can you take for granted you are not separated from the communion with the

---

7 Eucharistic Prayer III.

8 LG, no. 26.

9 J. Cardinal Ratzinger, "The Ecclesiology of Vatican II", in *L'Osservatore Romano* (November 25, 1985).

10 LG, no. 3: "In the sacrament of the Eucharist, the unity of believers who form one body in Christ is both expressed and brought about."

Christians of the whole world if, contrary to custom, you keep my name silent during the sacred mysteries?" [11]

We pray for all the bishops, for all priests, and for all of us who take part in this celebration. We pray for all who seek God with a sincere heart.

Intercessions for the dead

In the second section, we pray for those who have died in the peace of Christ.

How can we fail to remember here on earth this or that person so dear to us? Perhaps, during his lifetime, he did not seem to have as much faith as we would have liked to see in him. Hence, we find ourselves a bit concerned about his salvation. Therefore, we pray for all the dead whose faith, perhaps hidden to men's eyes, only God knew. [12]

In all Masses, the Church prays for the dead, so that on the basis of the communion existing among all of us as Christ's members, our petition for spiritual help may bring comforting hope for our faithful departed. [13] "We pray for our deceased forefathers and for all those who have lived among us. For we have a deep conviction that great help will be afforded those souls for whom prayers are offered while this holy and awesome Victim is present." [14]

At this moment, the priest may add a beautiful prayer for a deceased person whenever the Second or Third Eucharistic Prayer is used. He asks God to remember that person; since "in baptism he died with Christ, may he also share his resurrection, when Christ will raise our mortal bodies and make them like his own in glory." [15]

Seeking the intercession of the saints

Finally, the Intercessions have a third section to invoke the help of those brothers of ours now enjoying themselves in the glory of

[11] Pope Pelagius I, *Ep.* 5: PL 69:398c.
[12] Eucharistic Prayer IV.
[13] GIRM, no. 335.
[14] St. Cyril of Jerusalem, *Catechesis*, 23 [*Mystagogical* 5], 8–18: PG 33:1115.
[15] Eucharistic Prayer III.

heaven. We manifest also the desire of sharing with them the heavenly inheritance. "Celebrating the eucharistic sacrifice we are most
closely united to the Church in heaven in communion with and
venerating the memory first of all of the glorious ever-Virgin Mary,
of the blessed Joseph and the blessed apostles and martyrs and of all
the saints." [16]

The Intercessions in the Roman Canon

In the Roman Canon we find the three sections of the Intercessions
split into two fragments.[17] The first fragment was included in the
Epiclesis (before the Consecration) at around the fifth century.

INTERCESSION FOR THE LIVING
We offer them [these gifts we offer you in sacrifice]
  for your holy catholic Church,
watch over it, Lord, and guide it;
grant it peace and unity throughout the world.
We offer them for N., our Pope,
for N., our bishop,
and for all who hold and teach the catholic faith
that comes to us from the apostles.
Remember, Lord, your people,
especially those for whom we now pray,
N. and N.
Remember all of us gathered here before you.

---

[16] LG, no. 50.

[17] A letter of Pope Innocent I (401–417) gives us the reason for the interruption of
the Roman Canon and the insertion of the intercessory prayers: the desire to hear
within the Sacred Action (*inter mysteria sacra*) the names of those who are prayed for.
As to what determined its present position, we can only fall back on some theories, of
which Cardinal Schuster's appears to be the most plausible: While the celebrant commemorated the apostles and dead popes, the deacon began to read the list of names
(called *diptychs*) of the lay offerers; both ended their readings at the point at which
"Father, accept this offering" is said, before the Consecration. There the deacon
stopped, and, after the evangelical words of the Institution, again began the reading of
the diptychs, now having reached the list of names of the dead, which he concluded
while the celebrant, for his part, finished saying the Canon. See also G. Chevrot, *Our
Mass*, pp. 179–180.

You know how firmly we believe in you
and dedicate ourselves to you.
We offer you this sacrifice of praise
for ourselves and those who are dear to us.
We pray to you, our living and true God,
for our well-being and redemption.

INVOCATION TO THE SAINTS
In union with the whole Church
we honor Mary,
the ever-virgin mother of Jesus Christ our Lord and God.
We honor Joseph, her husband,
the apostles and martyrs
Peter and Paul, Andrew,
James, John, Thomas,
James, Philip,
Bartholomew, Matthew, Simon and Jude;
we honor Linus, Cletus, Clement, Sixtus,
Cornelius, Cyprian, Lawrence, Chrysogonus,
John and Paul, Cosmas and Damian
and all the saints.
May their merits and prayers
gain us your constant help and protection.
Through Christ our Lord. Amen.

Father, accept this offering
from your whole family.
Grant us your peace in this life,
save us from final damnation,
and count us among those you have chosen.
Through Christ our Lord. Amen.

We find in this prayer, first, the intercessions for the living members of the Church. The priest declares that the Church is *holy*, because we are sanctified by the water and the Holy Spirit. "The Church is called *catholic* or universal because she has spread throughout the entire world, from one end of the earth to the other. Again, she is called catholic because she teaches fully and unfailingly all the doctrine, . . . because she cures unrestrictedly every type of sin,

. . . and because she possesses within herself every kind of virtue that can be named." [18] She is "the sign or instrument both of a very closely knit union with God and of the unity of the whole human race." [19]

After asking for unity and beseeching God to preserve the Church from heresy and schism, it is natural that we pray for those whom the Holy Spirit has set as shepherds over the Church of God; the pope and our bishop.

All of us notice the praise given us in this passage. The priest tells God of us, "You know how firmly we *believe* in you and *dedicate* ourselves to you." God alone can read the consciences of men, but we desire always to be his faithful and loyal children and to do everything we can so as to obey his will, with piety and cheerfulness.

We then find the invocations to the saints. This last section dates from the third century. It includes, with obvious enthusiasm, a mention of "Mary, the ever-virgin mother of Jesus Christ," and St. Joseph. Then follow the names of the eleven apostles plus St. Paul and twelve martyrs held in special honor in Rome.[20] This first fragment ends with "Father, accept this offering . . ." It was affixed here by Pope St. Gregory about the year 600. It warns us of the imminent return to the Epiclesis or Invocation, which was interrupted earlier.

The second fragment of intercessory prayers in the Roman Canon is placed after the Consecration—specifically, between the Oblation and the Final Doxology.

---

[18] St. Cyril of Jerusalem, *Catechesis*, 18, 23–25: PG 33:1043.

[19] LG, no. 1. The term *catholic* was already used by St. Ignatius of Antioch (in 110). Its use in the Mass is attested by Optatus of Milevi (in 312); see CSEL 26:47.

[20] Perhaps we have heard little of them. Five popes head the list: St. Peter's three successors, Linus, Cletus, Clement; then two popes of the third century, Sixtus II and Cornelius; Cyprian, Bishop of Carthage, the intrepid defender of Catholic unity; the deacon Lawrence, who when his persecutor demanded from him the "treasures" of the Church, showed him hundreds of poor people; Chrysogonus, a Roman priest who carried out the holy work of comforting the Christians who were in prison; two brothers, John and Paul, both officers of the imperial palace, who were put to death under Julian the Apostate; and lastly, Cosmas and Damian, two Oriental physicians who gave their aid freely, and at whose graves there occurred "yet more cures than they had effected in their lives."

INTERCESSIONS FOR THE DEAD
Remember, Lord, those who have died
and have gone before us marked
with the sign of faith,
especially those for whom we now pray, N. and N.
May these, and all who sleep in Christ,
find in your presence
light, happiness, and peace.

INTERCESSIONS FOR THE LIVING
For ourselves, too, we ask
some share in the fellowship of your apostles and martyrs,
with John the Baptist, Stephen, Matthias, Barnabas,
Ignatius, Alexander, Marcellinus, Peter,
Felicity, Perpetua, Agatha, Lucy,
Agnes, Cecilia, Anastasia
and all the saints.
Though we are sinners,
we trust in your mercy and love.
Do not consider what we truly deserve,
but grant us your forgiveness.

The theme of intercession reappears here first to commend to the Lord his deceased servants. The priest uses expressions sounding as though they had been borrowed from the catacombs: "May these, and all who sleep in Christ, find in your presence light, happiness, and peace [*locum refrigerii, lucis et pacis*]." (The word "death" is not said in the presence of Christ, our eternal Life.)

Next, we ask for ourselves, using a prayer dating from the seventh century, or earlier. It begins with the expression, "*Nobis quoque peccatoribus famulis tuis*": "For ourselves, too . . . though we are sinners . . . ," we still are your children. While the priest strikes his breast at these words, we unprofitable servants call on our Father God, "Have mercy on me, a sinner!" (Lk 18:13).

The prayer continues with a second list of saints which completes that placed before the Consecration.[21] It seems that the first list of

---

[21] It mentions, in the first place, John (here obviously St. John the Baptist), and then seven men, followed by seven women, all martyrs. Stephen is the first deacon, whose

saints was not satisfying enough to Roman piety, which desired to fill certain gaps and make public mention of other saints venerated in the City. Thus, the Christians of Rome seized the opportunity of the remembrance of the dead to complete the first list. We ask God some share in their fellowship, humbly acknowledging, "Do not consider what we truly deserve, but grant us your forgiveness."

glorious martyrdom is recounted in the Acts of the Apostles (6:8–7:60). Two apostles come next: Matthias, elected to take the place of Judas (Acts 1:15–16) and probably left out of the first list so as not to exceed the number of twelve, and Barnabas, St. Paul's companion in his first missionary journey. Ignatius is the famous bishop of Antioch, sentenced to be fed to the wild beasts in Rome under Trajano. Besides their names and the place of their martyrdom, little else is known of Alexander, the priest Marcellinus, and the exorcist Peter, who were all put to death in the great persecution of Diocletian. The list continues with the names of the two young girls, Felicity and Perpetua (their names form the expression "everlasting happiness"), who confessed their faith at Carthage; and of Agatha and Lucy in Sicily. It concludes with the names of two young martyrs beloved by the Romans, Agnes and Cecilia; and of Anastasia, martyred at Sirmium and later honored in Rome.

29. The Final Doxology

To God, the only God, who saves us through Jesus Christ our Lord, be the glory, majesty, authority and power, which he had before time began, now and for ever. Amen (Jude 25).

In the Roman Canon, we find a short prayer which introduces the doxology: "Through him [Christ] you give us all these gifts," as spiritual nourishment and redemption. "You fill them with life and goodness," by means of the transubstantiation. "You bless them," because we receive abundant grace through this sacrament, "and make them holy."

This prayer marks the flow of divine gifts coming down to us through Christ. And then, in the Final Doxology, all praise and honor from the entire creation rise up to God through Christ.

All the Eucharistic Prayers end with the Final Doxology. It is a song of praise to God, beginning from the Preface. The priest takes the chalice and the paten with the host and, lifting them up, sings or says,

Through him, with him, in him,
in the unity of the Holy Spirit,
all glory and honor is yours, almighty Father,
for ever and ever.

These words are said by the priest alone.[1] Taken in part from St. Paul (Rom 11:36), they are to be found in the earliest forms of the Anaphora.[2] They are majestic in their simplicity.

---

[1] "On the other hand the assembly does not remain passive and inert: it unites itself to the priest in faith and silence and shows its concurrence by the various interventions provided for in the course of the Eucharistic Prayer: the responses to the Preface dialogue, the *Sanctus*, the acclamation after the Consecration, and the final *Amen* after the *Per Ipsum* [Through him . . .]. The *Per Ipsum* itself is reserved to the priest. This *Amen* especially should be emphasized by being sung, since it is the most important in the whole Mass" (ID, no. 4); see also GIRM, no. 55h *in fine*.

[2] *Didaché* (year 110), St. Justin (year 150), and the *Anaphora of St. Hippolytus* (d. 235).

Through him: Through Jesus' mediation, we have access to God. "No one can come to the Father except through me" (Jn 14:6), Jesus says. He introduces us to his Father; and on his account, the Father hears us favorably, forgives us, and loves us.

With him: We are children of God, through the adoption Christ merited for us, and, as a consequence, we are made his co-heirs. "Without me you can do nothing" (Jn 15:5), he says. With him, our lives will glorify God on the earth. On the altar, Jesus unites us to his perfect obedience. He wants us, throughout the whole day, to be with him in work and in prayer; he wants us to be his companions, in expiation and in apostolate.

In him: There is one and the same life in him and in us. "He who eats my flesh and drinks my blood lives in me and I live in him" (Jn 6:56), Christ says. So his life flows out into ours; from the Head to us as members of his Mystical Body. Our nothingness, our sins, our miseries are, as it were, absorbed by Christ, and they disappear in his infinite perfection. In him, too, we love our brothers and devote ourselves to their service.

In the unity of the Holy Spirit: The Church is a unity brought together by the Holy Spirit.[3] He joins us together as believers and gives us the life of grace by which we become children of God. He dwells in us, enabling us to offer the sacrifice of praise to God, together with the entire Church.

The people's acclamation *Amen* is an assent and a conclusion.[4] Our offering, which is Christ's offering on the cross, calls for a unanimous and enthusiastic *Amen*.

Already in the third century, the Christian people were granted these privileges: "To hear the Eucharistic Prayer, to acclaim the final Amen, to go to the sacred table, to receive the divine Bread." [5]

---

[3] LG, no. 13.
[4] GIRM, no. 55h.
[5] Dennis of Alexandria (d. 265), in Eusebius, *Historia eccl.*, VII, 9: PG 20:656.

Let us sing or say the Great Amen with all our hearts united to all our brothers. Let it resound the whole world over, as the Amen of our early brothers in the faith "resounded in heaven, as a celestial thunderclap in the Roman basilicas." [6]

This is the most important Amen in the Mass. It is for us both a resolution and a prayer. A resolution upon which our love for God blooms; a prayer based on the future hope of resurrection.

As THE priest holds the paten and chalice, let us remember that Mary also held her Son's body after the crucifixion. Together with our Mother, Mother of the Church, we unite ourselves to the offering of the Church.

---

[6] St. Jerome, *In Gal. comment.*: *"ad similitudinem caelestis tonitrui Amen reboat."*

PART IV
LITURGY OF THE EUCHARIST (*Continued*)

C. Communion Rite

We all stand even as the Great Amen, uniting us to the sacred action, still echoes in the church.

The ancient sacrificial custom required that part of the victim be given back to the person offering the sacrifice. Thus, he became, symbolically, God's guest. That which was just a symbol in the pagan rites and a figure in the Jewish offerings, is a reality in the Holy Mass. After we have offered to God his Son Jesus Christ in sacrifice, God offers him to us as spiritual food.[1]

ONCE they were set free from the oppression of the Egyptians, the Jews had to travel across the desert. Their confidence in God began to dwindle. They began to complain against Moses, "You have brought us to this wilderness to starve to death!" (Ex 16:3). But God's patience was greater than the nasty complaints of the Israelites. He sent them manna, "bread from heavens." Each morning for forty years, until they entered the Promised Land, the people went out and gathered the day's portion of manna; only for the Sabbath rest did they get a double portion.

Jesus himself pointed out the manna as a prefiguration of the Eucharist: "Your fathers ate the manna in the desert and they are dead; but this is the bread that comes down from heaven, so that a man may eat it and not die" (Jn 6:49). The Christians are strengthened by the body of Christ, the true "Bread from heaven," during their pilgrimage on earth, in the same way that the Jews were nourished during their wandering in the desert. If the manna was a token of God's tender care for the chosen people whom he delivered from slavery, more so does the Eucharist reveal God's paternal love for us. Those who nourish their soul with the Eucharist, the body and blood of Christ, can be sure of reaching the end of the road that leads to eternal life.

---

[1] Georges Chevrot, *Our Mass*, p. 218.

The early Christians always likened the Eucharist to the life of the soul. St. Augustine writes:

> It is an excellent thing that the Christians around Carthage call baptism itself nothing else but salvation, and the sacrament of Christ's body nothing else but life. By apostolic tradition the churches of Christ hold that without baptism and participation at the Lord's table it is impossible for any man to attain either the kingdom of God or salvation and life eternal. The Scriptures give testimony of this.[2]

In the synagogue of Capernaum, Jesus said,

> "I am the bread of life. Your fathers ate the manna in the desert and they are dead. . . . I am the living bread which has come down from heaven. Anyone who eats this bread will live for ever; and the bread that I shall give is my flesh, for the life of the world" (Jn 6:48ff.).

These words perplexed those who heard Christ. They had followed him after the multiplication of the fishes and the loaves. This promise of living bread . . . , his flesh . . . , his blood . . . , sounded like madness. The Lord did not take back his assertions; he even went further on with a cascade of declarations. The spiral of surprises reached the point of scandal when he assured them:

> "I tell you most solemnly, if you do not eat the flesh of the Son of Man and drink his blood, you will not have life in you. Anyone who does eat my flesh and drink my blood has eternal life, and I shall raise him up on the last day. . . . He who eats my flesh and drinks my blood lives in me and I in him" (Jn 6:53ff.).

After this, St. John notes, many left him and stopped going with him.

During the Last Supper, Jesus redeemed his promise, making it a reality, to the amazement of the apostles. "What we cannot do, our

---

[2] *De baptismo parvulorum*, 1, 24, 34.

Lord is able to do. Jesus Christ, perfect God and perfect man, leaves us, not a symbol, but a reality. He himself stays with us. He will go to the Father, but he will also remain among men. He will leave us, not simply a gift that will make us remember him, not an image that becomes blurred with time, like a photograph that soon fades and yellows, and has no meaning except for those who were contemporaries. Under the appearances of bread and wine, he is really present, with his body and blood, with his soul and divinity." [3]

This is the very same body and blood which, by being immolated, restored our friendship with God. Christ's sacrifice and the paschal meal are intimately linked. Our Mother the Church encourages us to participate in one and in the other, if we are properly disposed,[4] by receiving our Lord's body and blood. These will be our nourishment for the journey to our Father's home. And this is what the Communion rite is going to do: to prepare our soul to receive our Lord.

IN THE early Church, the Communion rite was simple. The Anaphora was followed by the Breaking of the Bread, and then by the Lord's Prayer and Communion. A crown of prayers and ceremonies was added through the centuries. Nowadays, the Communion rite is ordained thus:

- Lord's Prayer, preceded by the invitation to pray and followed by the Embolism[5] and the people's acclamation.

- Rite of Peace.

- Breaking of the Bread, with the Commingling, while the *Agnus Dei* is said or sung.

- Personal preparation of the priest.

- Invitation to the sacred banquet by showing the host to the faithful.

- Communion of the priest and the faithful.

---

[3] J. Escrivá de Balaguer, *Christ Is Passing By*, no. 83.
[4] GIRM, no. 56.
[5] *Embolism* means "extension."

- Communion song.
- Silent prayer, if opportune.
- Prayer after Communion.

30. *The Lord's Prayer*

"You should pray like this: Our Father in heaven . . ."
(Mt 6:9–13).

The priest offers the invitation to pray, and all of us continue the prayer with him. The priest raises his hands. No special gesture is indicated for the people during this prayer.

This invitation is a very touching and most ancient formula (one alluded to as early as the fourth century by St. Jerome). It states that we should not dare (*audemus*) to utter what we are about to say—were it not for the express command of our Lord. He taught us to approach God as a son talks to his father. Hence, the priest says:

Jesus taught us to call God our Father
and so we have the courage to say . . .

or

Let us pray with confidence to the Father
in the words our Savior gave us . . .

The profound religious atmosphere pervading the Canon is increased here with the great reverence rendered to this prayer. We are so miserable, and our mind is so limited, that we do not even know what we should ask of God. Jesus Christ himself deigned to compose this prayer to indicate how we should address God. It is our Savior's own prayer and, therefore, the prayer of the Christian.

In the early Church, the Lord's Prayer was taught to the catechumens only a few weeks before baptism. Outside the Mass, it was always said in a low voice. It seemed that the faithful recited it before Communion, which they took home on Sundays and received there on ordinary days. Then, it may have been introduced into the Mass. Many are the allusions made to this custom in the writings of the Fathers of the Church, and St. Augustine regarded it as something well established in his own time.

Our Father. Our Lord used the Aramaic word *Abba*. It is how children called their father; the best translation could be "Daddy." God wants us to deal with him with full confidence, as his little children. All our prayer is nourished by this fact; we are children of God.

How merciful the Lord is to us, how kind and richly compassionate! He wished us to repeat this prayer in God's sight, to call the Lord our Father and, as Christ is God's Son, be called in turn sons of God! None of us would ever have dared to utter this name unless he himself had allowed us to pray in this way.

We pray the Lord's Prayer, feeling ourselves members of the big family of the children of God, gathered in Christ by the Holy Spirit. "We are children of God, bearers of the only flame that can light up the paths of the earth for souls, of the only brightness which can never be darkened, dimmed, or overshadowed.

"The Lord uses us as torches, to make that light shine out. Much depends on us; if we respond many people will remain in darkness no longer, but will walk instead along paths that lead to eternal life." [1]

During the day, we can ponder each of the seven petitions of the Lord's Prayer. These will give us abundant material for our prayer and meditation.

Hallowed be thy name. It is not that we think to make God holy by our prayers; rather we are asking God that his name may be made holy in us. Indeed, how could God be made holy, he who is the source of holiness? Still, because he himself said, "Be holy, for I am holy," we pray and ask him that we who have been hallowed in baptism may persevere in what we have begun. In the first petition, we desire to obtain the highest degree of sanctity for all. We desire to give glory to God: that he may be loved and feared by all; that his holiness, his goodness, and his wisdom may be acknowledged everywhere.

Thy kingdom come. In the second petition, we desire that God may reign in everybody's will. We ask that we all may happily reach our destination in his kingdom. We pray that the kingdom promised to us by God will come, the kingdom won by Christ's blood and passion. Then we who formerly were slaves in this world will reign from now on under the dominion of Christ, in accordance with his promise: "Come, O blessed of my Father, receive the kingdom which was prepared for you from the foundation of the world."

---

[1] J. Escrivá de Balaguer, *The Forge*, no. 1.

Thy will be done on earth as it is in heaven. In the third petition, we pray that all men serve and obey God on earth as he is served by the angels in heaven; and that all may always avoid sin and do what is pleasing to God. We do not pray that God should do his will, but that we may carry out his will. How could anyone prevent the Lord from doing what he wills? But in our prayer we ask that God's will be done in us, because the devil throws up obstacles to prevent our mind and our conduct from obeying God in all things. So if his will is to be done in us we have need of his will, that is, his help and protection. No one can be strong by his own strength or secure save by God's mercy and forgiveness.

Give us this day our daily bread. In the fourth petition, we ask for whatever is necessary for nourishment, clothing, and other temporal needs; for our daily food, which for a Christian means also the body of Christ, and for the forgiveness of sins.[2] Thus, we can understand this petition in a spiritual and in a literal sense. For in the divine plan both senses may help toward our salvation. Christ is the bread of life; this bread does not belong to everyone, but is ours alone. We who want to live in Christ and receive the Eucharist, the food of salvation, ask for this bread to be given us every day. With Christ's help, we who live and abide in him will never be separated from his body and his grace.

Forgive us our trespasses as we forgive those who trespass against us. Once we have requested the needed sustenance from God's magnanimity, we ask him pardon for our sins. To be reminded that we are sinners and forced to ask forgiveness for our faults is prudent and sound. Even while we are asking God's forgiveness, our hearts are aware of our state! This command to pray daily for our sins reminds us that we commit sin every day. No one should complacently think himself innocent, lest his pride lead to further sin.

Christ clearly laid down an additional rule. Thus we are made aware that we cannot obtain what we ask regarding our own trespasses unless we do the same for those who trespass against us. This is why he says elsewhere: "The measure you give will be the measure you get." And the servant who, after his master forgives all his debt, refuses to forgive his fellow servant is thrown into prison. Because he

---

[2] GIRM, no. 56a.

refused to be kind to his fellow servant, he lost the favor his master had given him. We make an act of contrition and of sincere love toward our enemies and all who have caused us any harm. We wholeheartedly love them in the Lord.

Lead us not into temptation. In the sixth petition, we ask God to keep us from falling into temptations. We should not trust our own strength; we should fear our malice and lack of constancy, lest these induce us to wander away from his grace and friendship.

Deliver us from evil. In the seventh petition, we ask for deliverance from the evils which afflict us and may set us away from his fatherly love. Our hearts are filled with hope as we remember the Lord telling the disciples, "What father among you would hand his son a stone when he asked for bread?" (Lk 11:11). We ask to be liberated from the guilt and punishment of sin, from all snares that the devil and the world set up against us.[3]

Now, we are going to recite the Lord's Prayer before Communion. It will suffice for us to savor these petitions with our hearts turned toward our Father and our brothers. We will, then, realize we love them more than we think we do. And relying on their help, we will feel safe. It is logical: "A brother helped by his brother is a fortress" (Prov 18:19).

Meanwhile, the priest alone develops the last petition of the Lord's Prayer in the Embolism. He begs, on behalf of all of us, for deliverance from the power of evil:

> *Deliver us, Lord, from every evil,*
> *and grant us peace in our day.*
> *In your mercy keep us free from sin*
> *and protect us from all anxiety*
> *as we wait in joyful hope*
> *for the coming of our Savior, Jesus Christ.*

We join in that petition with our acclamation, which is also a doxology or hymn of praise to God:

> *For the kingdom, the power, and the glory are yours, now and for ever.*[4]

---

[3] St. Cyprian of Carthage (200–258), *The Lord's Prayer*, 12–18; see also J. Cardinal Bona (seventeenth century), *De Sacrificio Missae*, v, 10.

[4] Taken from the *Didaché* (*Teaching of the Twelve Apostles*) (year 110), ch. 10.

31. *The Rite of Peace*

"This is my commandment: love one another, as I have loved you" (Jn 15:12).

Before we share the same spiritual food, we implore peace and unity for the Church and for the whole human family and offer some sign of our love for one another.[1]

Communion is getting closer, and the liturgy becomes ever more intimate. While all the preceding prayers of the Mass were directed to God the Father, now for the first time after the rite of washing his hands the priest addresses himself directly to Jesus Christ. With his hands extended, he prays for peace:

> *Lord Jesus Christ, you said to your apostles:*
> *I leave you peace, my peace I give you.*
> *Look not on our sins, but on the faith of your Church,*
> *and grant us the peace and unity of your kingdom*
> *where you live for ever and ever.*

When we pronounce our "Amen," we must realize that we are asking not only for our personal peace but also for peace for the whole Church. We know that "every kingdom divided against itself is heading for ruin; and a household divided against itself collapses" (Lk 11:17). What a good moment now to rectify, lest the Lord find us at war with one another under the flimsy excuse of serving him better!

This is a good moment to exert effort and begin to understand the reasons and attitudes of others, no matter how different they may be from ours; to love pluralism in the nondogmatic issues; to respect the diverse viewpoints in debatable matters. How often do we try to proffer our personal solution, passing it as the Gospel message, though it really remains just that: one more private opinion. Here is a reminder from the Second Vatican Council:

---

[1] GIRM, no. 56b.

It is necessary for people to remember that no one is allowed in these situations to appropriate the Church's authority for his opinion.[2]

With these good dispositions, we receive the priest's greeting:

The peace of the Lord be with you always.

The priest gives us the greeting of peace while extending and then joining his hands. "And also with you," we respond. Then, if the opportunity warrants it,[3] the priest may add:

Let us offer each other the sign of peace.

We all exchange some sign of peace and love, according to local custom: shaking hands, or, in some countries, bowing our heads.

DURING the Last Supper, our Lord made his disciples aware of the importance of peace, the fruit of charity. Many times he spoke of unity, of the spirit of service, of humility, of charity. These are virtues and dispositions of the soul which can thrive only in an atmosphere of peace. Jesus then made a gesture of profound humility which left Peter and the other apostles surprised and confused. "Jesus got up from table, removed his outer garment and, taking a towel, wrapped it round his waist; he then poured water into a basin and began to wash the disciples' feet and to wipe them with the towel he was wearing."

The Lord's action and attire were those of a slave. He himself explained the meaning of this act of humility: "If I, then, the Lord and Master, have washed your feet, you should wash each other's feet. I have given you an example so that you may copy what I have done to you" (Jn 13:4–15).

We, his disciples, are invited to love and serve others, and not be afraid of placing ourselves last. In the Eucharist, the sacrament of love, the Lord gives himself to us in sacrifice. His love impels him to lay down his life for us. We receive from this sacrament the strength

---

[2] GS, 43.

[3] "Pro opportunitate"; see *Missale Romanum* (editio typica altera 1981); GIRM, no. 112.

to commit ourselves to a life of service and dedication to others, to spread around the peace and love of God.

Humility, charity, and spirit of service, as we said earlier, are virtues and dispositions of the soul which can thrive only in an atmosphere of peace. After his resurrection, Jesus appeared to the disciples and, to make this point clear, greeted them, "Peace be with you" (Jn 20:20).

The early Christians lived well this point of their spirit. St. Paul bore witness of their charity and unity, at times greeting them with the symbolic kiss of peace.[4] And so it entered the ancient liturgy. First, the rite of peace was set at the end of the Mass of the catechumens (before the Offertory). It followed the Prayer of the Faithful and, at that point, could be seen as a sign of love before the gifts were offered. Perhaps it was placed there in reminiscence of this passage in the Gospel:

> If you are bringing your offering to the altar and there remember that your brother has something against you, leave your offering there before the altar, go and be reconciled with your brother first, and then come back and present your offering (Mt 5:23–24).

At the time of Pope St. Innocent I (401–417), this rite became an obligatory prelude to Communion, "as a sign of the people's acquiescence in all that had been done in these mysteries." Thus the petition of the Lord's Prayer, "Forgive us our trespasses as we forgive those who trespass against us," was carried into effect. At any rate, it would be fitting for us to examine our conscience, just in case anything is left that may be in need of purification.

CERTAINLY the Lord wants us fraternally united in an environment of supernatural and human peace. Only then can our love of God and men grow. Pope Paul VI thus advises the priests:

> The sacrament of the Eucharist is a sign and cause of the unity of Christ's Mystical Body, and because it stirs up an active "ecclesial" spirit in those who are more fervent in

---

[4] Rom 16:16; 1 Cor 16:20; 2 Cor 13:12; 1 Thes 5:26.

their eucharistic devotion, never stop urging your faithful, as they approach the mystery of the Eucharist, to learn to embrace the Church's cause as their own, to pray to God without slackening, to offer themselves to God as an acceptable sacrifice for the peace and unity of the Church; so that all the sons of the Church may be united and feel united and there may be no divisions among them but rather unity of mind and intention.[5]

We feel our soul flooded with peace; that is the consequence of our divine filiation and a fraternity well lived, centered in Christ. Men lose their peace when they lack this filiation and fraternity. "I realize I am a son of God; if the Lord is my light and my salvation, whom should I fear?"

Here is a thought that brings peace and that the Holy Spirit provides ready-made for those who seek the will of God: *"Dominus regit me, et nihil mihi deerit"*—"The Lord rules me, and I shall want nothing."
What can upset a soul who sincerely repeats these words? [6]

And so, we abandon ourselves completely in God's will:

An act of complete correspondence to the will of God: Is that what you want, Lord? . . . Then it's what I want also! [7]

A determined resolution to fulfill the will of God in the smallest things is the only way we can be truly happy. The relative happiness we can achieve here on earth shall be made complete in heaven.

5 MF, no. 70.
6 J. Escrivá de Balaguer, *The Way*, no. 760.
7 Escrivá, *The Way*, no. 762.

32. *The Breaking of the Bread and the* Agnus Dei

Seeing Jesus coming toward him, John said, "Look, there is the lamb of God that takes away the sin of the world" (Jn 1:29).

Breaking of the Bread

As practiced before and now, the priest takes the host and breaks it over the paten. He places a small piece into the chalice while saying,

May this mingling of the body and blood of our Lord Jesus Christ bring eternal life to us who receive it.

The breaking of the loaf of bread is a familiar ceremony in countries where bread is the staple food. The father, presiding over the table, would perform the ceremony, the origin of which harks back to the very beginning of mankind.

At the Last Supper, our Lord also broke the bread (the Jews always *broke*, and never *cut*, their bread). It was in the act of breaking bread that the risen Lord was recognized by the disciples at Emmaus. As if it were a Mass celebrated by the Lord, the breaking of the bread was preceded by the liturgy of the word: While they were walking, "Jesus explained to them the passages throughout the Scriptures that were about himself." Then, "while he was with them at table, he took the bread and said the blessing; then he broke it and handed it to them. And their eyes were opened and they recognized him" (Lk 24:27, 30–31).

The two disciples returned to Jerusalem, announcing that they had recognized the Lord "at the breaking of the bread."

In apostolic times, this gesture of Christ gave the entire eucharistic action its name, the *Breaking of the Bread*. We see, in the Acts of the Apostles, St. Luke writing that the Christians "were persevering in the doctrine of the apostles, and in the communication of the breaking of the bread, and in prayers" (Acts 2:42).

St. Paul drew a lesson from the fact that all those present shared of the same loaf:

The fact that there is only one loaf means that, though there are many of us, we form a single body because we all have a share in this one loaf (1 Cor 10:17).

While the bread used in it was unleavened, this ceremony also had a practical reason: the need of breaking the big loaf of bread by the deacon before its distribution. We read in the *Didaché* (year 110):

Lord, just as the matter of this bread was scattered on the hills and was made one when it was gathered together, so too may your Church be gathered in one into your kingdom from the ends of the earth.[1]

And St. Cyprian, in laying stress on the Church's unity in opposition to schism, wrote:

The Lord's sacrifice proclaims the unity of Christians, who are bound together by a firm and unshakeable charity. For when the Lord calls the bread, which has been made from many grains of wheat, his body, he is describing our people whose unity he has sustained; and when he refers to wine pressed from many grapes and berries as his blood, once again he is speaking of our flock which has been formed by fusing many into one.[2]

IN THE ancient Church, some fragments of consecrated hosts were reserved. Two of these were called *sancta* and *fermentum*. The *sancta* was to be consumed at the next Mass to be celebrated; it was dropped into the chalice. This gesture seemed to have meant the affirmation of the unity of the sacrifice of Jesus Christ until the end of the world.

The sacrifice of Calvary, renewed at different times in different places, is the Church's universal sacrifice and eternal prayer. It is everywhere the same. This was emphasized in the ancient papal Mass by the reservation and dispatching of the *fermentum* ("yeast"). The pope or

---

[1] *Didaché*, ch. 9.
[2] *Epistle to Magnus*, 6: PL 3:1139.

bishop sent fragments of the hosts he had consecrated to priests of the nearby parishes, "so that," Pope Innocent I (401–417) explained, "especially on this day, they do not think themselves cut off from our communion." As the yeast binds the dough and makes one whole of it, so the Eucharist is the bond between the pastor and the members of his flock; it is also a sign of the unity of the priesthood.[3]

As YESTERDAY, the entire people of God is now united around the altar for the eucharistic sacrifice celebrated by the ordinary shepherd of the community, and receives the sacrament from his hands.[4] Nevertheless, we should not give undue emphasis to the communitarian aspect, leaving in the second place the most important fact: Our Lord, really present, is the link in this unity.

> But the Church is not brought into being only through the union of people, through the experience of brotherhood to which the eucharistic banquet gives rise. The Church is brought into being when, in that fraternal union and communion, we celebrate the sacrifice of the cross of Christ, when we proclaim "the Lord's death until he comes" (1 Cor 11:26); and later, when, being compenetrated with the mystery of salvation, we approach as a community the table of the Lord, in order to be nourished there, in a sacramental manner, by the fruits of the holy sacrifice of propitiation. Therefore, in eucharistic Communion we receive Christ, Christ himself; and our union with him, which is a gift and grace for each individual, brings it about that in him we are also associated in the unity of his Body which is the Church.[5]

The Commingling

The origin of the custom of placing a fragment of the consecrated host into the chalice is not exactly known. Some say that the separated species signify the Victim in state of death (the body in one

---

[3] Georges Chevrot, *Our Mass*, pp. 119–200.

[4] LG, no. 26; Second Vatican Council, decree *Christus Dominus*, no. 11.

[5] DC, no. 4.

place, the blood in another), whereas in reality our Lord is present in either and in both species, as he is in heaven, living and glorious. Therefore, the mingling symbolizes the re-union of Christ's body and soul as in his resurrection. It is, however, probable that the mingling must have corresponded to the dogmatic need of showing clearly the unity and indivisibility of the body and blood of Jesus Christ.

Agnus Dei

During the breaking of the bread and the commingling, the *Agnus Dei* is sung or said by all:

> *Lamb of God, you take away the sins of the world:*
> *have mercy on us.*

The final phrase is always: "Grant us peace."

At first, the breaking of the bread was done in silence. It was a Syrian pope, St. Sergius I (687–701), who established the singing of this invocation. He had been familiar with it since childhood. Christ is shown not only to be present, but also as Victim.

The figure of the "Lamb of God" is full of meaning and is helpful to enkindle our devotion before Communion. The Lamb foretold by Isaiah and announced by St. John the Baptist should wipe out our sins through his obedience to God's will:

> Innocent, he never opened his mouth,
> like a lamb that is led to the slaughter house,
> like a sheep that is dumb before its shearers (Is 53:7).

Let us make up with a great longing to atone for our sins and be cleansed for our lack of innocence.

But this Lamb was also foreshadowed by the paschal lamb the Jews sacrificed on the eve of their departure from their slavery in Egypt.

The expression of John the Baptist reminds us of the lamb with which the Jews celebrated the Passover every year, the pledge of the reconciliation of man with God. St. John the Evangelist, who was at the foot of the cross, observed that Jesus' legs were not broken as in the case of the two thieves. We find in this detail some similarity with that prescription of God for the paschal lamb: "You must not break any bone of it" (Ex 12:46).

Jesus is bought with silver coins coming from the alms destined to buy the lambs for the daily sacrifices, and he dies at the hour in which the paschal lamb used to be sacrificed in the Temple.

Finally, the *Agnus Dei* is also a nuptial hymn to celebrate the wedding of the Lamb with his bride, the Church, in peace and unity, as is described in the Book of Revelation. There, on the altar, the Lamb lies alive, but as if slain. Twenty-four elders are around the Lamb. They are clothed in white robes and crowned with gold. Thousands of angels hymn the sacrifice and triumph of the Lamb. Certainly, each Mass is only a prelude and a token of the future adoration of the Lamb in eternity.

33. *Immediate Preparation for Communion*

"Anyone who eats this bread will live for ever; and the bread that I shall give is my flesh, for the life of the world" (Jn 6:51).

In the early ages of the Church, no special prayer was designated as a preparation for Communion. The Eucharistic Prayer and the Lord's Prayer were sufficient. Our Mother the Church saw it fitting, nevertheless, to offer two prayers of preparation for the coming of the Lord to the temple which is our body. These prayers are of Gallican origin, dating from about the tenth century. They are full of fervor, rather subjective in tone, and suited for private piety, since they are intended as a personal preparation for the priest who recites one of them.

In the first prayer, the priest begs Christ, Son of the living God, to grant salvation to his servant and to deliver him from all his sins and from every evil. "Keep me faithful to your teaching, and never let me be parted from you," he ends.

In the other, the priest declares his own unworthiness and his confidence in Christ's mercy. He asks that the reception of the Eucharist may work not to his condemnation but to his own good.

The personal preparation of the priest gives us the opportunity to prepare ourselves also in silence, without the noise of words but with an abundance of acts of love. We feel unworthy as the moment for receiving our Lord approaches. But we decide to go on because we know he wants to remain in the consecrated species to be our nourishment and the cure for our weaknesses.

WE SHOULD never dare to receive the Eucharist in a state of mortal sin. To do so is to abuse sacrilegiously the mercy of God. Only a shallow and false love, based on mere sentimentality, can bring us to such a detestable course of action. This mistreatment of the sacrament is a grave offense against God.

St. Paul's warning on this issue is quite clear:

Anyone who eats the bread or drinks the cup of the Lord unworthily will be behaving unworthily toward the body and blood of the Lord. Everyone is to recollect himself before eating this bread and drinking this cup; because a person who eats and drinks without recognizing the body is eating and drinking his own condemnation (1 Cor 11:27–29).

And Pope John Paul II warns us:

We find in recent years the following phenomenon. Sometimes, indeed quite frequently, everybody participating in the eucharistic assembly goes to Communion; and on some such occasions, as experienced pastors confirm, there has not been due care to approach the sacrament of penance so as to purify one's conscience. This can of course mean that those approaching the Lord's table find nothing on their conscience, according to the objective law of God, to keep them from this sublime and joyful act of being sacramentally united with Christ. But there can also be, at least at times, another idea behind this: the idea of the Mass as *only* a banquet[1] in which one shares by *receiving the body of Christ in order to manifest, above all else, fraternal communion.* It is not hard to add to these reasons a certain human respect and mere "conformity." [2]

Therefore, we cannot—and should not—receive our Lord with a soul dirtied by sin. If we realize we have a serious sin, even though we may seem to be contrite, we cannot go and receive the Holy Eucharist without previous sacramental confession.[3]

IT IS interesting to notice the connection among the sacraments, specifically between the sacraments of Penance and the Eucharist. John Paul II points out:

---

[1] GIRM, nos. 7–8; *Missale Romanum*, ed. typica altera 1975, p. 29.

[2] DC, no. 11.

[3] Sacred Congregation of Divine Worship, *Holy Communion and Worship of the Eucharist Outside the Mass*, no. 23; cf. Council of Trent, Denz., no. 880.

The two sacraments of Reconciliation and the Eucharist remain closely linked. Without a continually renewed conversion and the reception of the sacramental grace of forgiveness, participation in the Eucharist would not reach its full redemptive efficacy.[4]

It is not only that Penance leads to the Eucharist, but that the Eucharist also leads to Penance. For when we realize who it is that we receive in eucharistic Communion, there springs up almost spontaneously a sense of unworthiness, together with sorrow for our own sins and an interior need for purification.[5]

We do not believe those who, challenging the teaching of our Lord, say that "they confess directly to God." That act of atonement is good in itself but incomplete. If they are really sincere, they should put into action their desire for atonement by receiving the sacrament of Penance. As the Lord commanded the apostles and their successors:

"For those whose sins you forgive, they are forgiven; for those whose sins you retain, they are retained" (Jn 20:23).

[4] John Paul II, *Letter of Holy Thursday* (1986), no. 8.
[5] DC, no. 7.

34. *The Communion of the Priest and the Faithful*

The centurion replied, "Sir, I am not worthy to have you under my roof; just give the word and my servant will be cured" (Mt 8:8).

The priest genuflects. Taking the host, he raises it slightly over the paten, showing it for Communion to the faithful. He says aloud,

This is the Lamb of God
who takes away the sins of the world.
Happy are those who are called to his supper.

This invitation to share in the sacred meal contains almost the same words used by John the Baptist (Jn 1:29) when he pointed out to John and Andrew the presence of the Lord among men.

Together with the priest, we continue with the same words of the centurion at Capernaum (Mt 8:8), to confess our unworthiness:

Lord, I am not worthy to receive you,
but only say the word and I shall be healed.

With gratitude, we declare our wonder before this great gift of God; with confidence, we tell our Lord to prepare our poor hearts. We would like the centurion's faith, humility, and simplicity at least to make our Lord as happy as in that incident.

After having taken Communion under the two species, the priest takes the paten or ciborium and goes to the communicants.[1] He raises the consecrated host slightly and shows it to each one, saying, "The body of Christ." The communicants reply, "Amen," and receive the sacrament.[2]

During the priest's and the faithful's reception of the sacrament, the Communion song is sung. Its function is to express outwardly the communicants' union in spirit by means of the unity of their

[1] "It is most desirable that the faithful receive the Lord's body from hosts consecrated at the same Mass . . ." (GIRM, no. 56h). Communion under both kinds is granted by the bishops not only to clerics, but also to the laity on certain occasions.

[2] GIRM, no. 117.

voices, to give evidence of the joy in their hearts, and to make the procession for the reception of Christ's body more fully an act of the community. The song begins when the priest takes Communion and continues for as long as it seems appropriate while the faithful receive Christ's body. But the Communion song should be ended in good time whenever there is to be a hymn after Communion.

If there is no singing, the Communion Antiphon in the missal is recited either by the people, by some of them, or by a reader. Otherwise, the priest himself says it after he has received Communion and before he gives Communion to the faithful.[3]

The Church has always required from the faithful respect and reverence for the Eucharist at the moment of receiving it. The Church's prescription and the evidence of the early Fathers make it abundantly clear. St. Cyril of Jerusalem (314–386), instructing the newly baptized, writes, "Come forward also to the cup of his blood, not reaching out with your hands, but bowing and in attitude of worship and reverence." [4] And St. Augustine exhorts, "Let no one eat the body of Christ without first adoring it." [5] It has been the custom in the Church since the olden times to receive the sacred host kneeling, according to the human way of acting, because this genuflection expresses adoration. More recently, we have been told:

> With regard to the manner of going to Communion, the faithful can receive it either kneeling or standing, in accordance with the norms laid down by the Bishop's Conference. "When the faithful communicate kneeling, no other sign of reverence toward the Blessed Sacrament is required, since kneeling is itself a sign of adoration. When they receive Communion standing, it is strongly recommended that, coming up in procession, they should make a sign of reverence before receiving the sacrament. This should be done at the right time and place, so that the order of people going to and from Communion is not disrupted." [6]

[3] GIRM, no. 56i.

[4] St. Cyril of Jerusalem, *Catechesis Mystagogical*, 5, 22.

[5] St. Augustine, *Enarrat. in Ps.* 98, 9.

[6] ID, no. 11. The quotation is from the Sacred Congregation of Rites, *Eucharisticum Mysterium*, no. 34; see also GIRM, 244c, 246b, 247b.

For many centuries, Holy Communion had been distributed by having it placed directly on the tongue. This practice is still in force.[7] It expresses the faithful's reverence for the Eucharist, and it is the best way to avoid any profanation. To receive Holy Communion in this way does not detract in any way from personal dignity; rather, it is part of the preparation needed to receive the Eucharist fruitfully.

When the bishops, with the approval of the Holy See, authorize in their territory the reception of Holy Communion in the hand, the faithful need to be instructed on the doctrine of the real presence of our Lord in the eucharistic species. Thus, we avoid any danger of profanation resulting from dispersing the fragments which perhaps break off the hosts, or from not having clean hands, and so on. One cannot say it doesn't matter if these particles stick to the communicants' fingers and end up in pockets or bags containing cigarettes, bubble gum, or lipstick. That would be a glaring lack of reverence for the body of the Lord. Worship implies reverence. Whatever hinders reverence hinders worship.

The same law points out that Communion in the hand can never be imposed in such a way as to exclude or make difficult the traditional usage. And even where the practice of Holy Communion in the hand is lawfully allowed, each Catholic is free to decide on whether he or she will receive the Eucharist in the mouth or in the hand.[8]

In the optional rite of Communion in the hand the communicant should place his cupped left palm upon the right. The minister places the sacred host on the left palm. Stepping aside yet still facing the minister, the communicant conveys the sacred host to his mouth with the right hand. The minister should ascertain that the host is consumed there.

The *Amen* that the communicant pronounces upon receiving the sacred host is equivalent to saying, "Yes, Lord, I believe. I love you and hope in you. I know my time of waiting is over, for my hope is now made into a reality which fulfills the deepest needs of my faith and my charity. You are mine, and I am yours, wholly made one in this sacrament. My soul worships you in stillness."

---

[7] Paul VI, instruction *Memoriale Domini*, May 24, 1969.
[8] Paul VI, *Memoriale Domini*; also his instruction *Immensae Caritatis*, January 29, 1973.

The catechism of the Council of Trent makes the following assertion:

> It is not the sacrament which changes, as would bread and wine, into our substance, it is, on the contrary, we ourselves who are changed, so to speak, into its nature. So that we can very well apply here those words of St. Augustine put into the mouth of our Lord: "I am the food of the strong, believe and you will eat me. But you will not change me into you, as you do with the food of your body, it is you who will be changed into me." [9]

Nevertheless, there is always the danger of our getting used to it and not paying due respect to our Lord present in the sacrament. Our Mother the Church has issued directives which help us to deal with our Lord with exquisite propriety and affection:

> Communion is a gift of God, given to the faithful through the minister appointed for this purpose. It is not permitted that the faithful should themselves pick up the consecrated bread and the sacred chalice; still less that they should hand them from one to another.
>
> The faithful, whether religious or lay, who are authorized as extraordinary ministers of the Eucharist can distribute Communion only when there is no priest, deacon or acolyte, when the priest is impeded by illness or advanced age, or when the number of the faithful going to Communion is so large as to make the celebration of Mass excessively long.[10] Accordingly, a reprehensible attitude is shown by those priests who, though present at the celebration, refrain from distributing Communion and leave this task to the laity.[11]

[9] Part II: The Eucharist, Effects. The quotation is from St. Augustine, *Confessions*, VII, c. 18.

[10] Sacred Congregation for the Discipline of the Sacraments, instruction *Immensae Caritatis* (January 29, 1973), no. 1.

[11] ID, 9–10.

This is so because the *ordinary ministers* for the distribution of Holy Communion are the bishop, the priests, and the deacons.[12] The acolyte is an *extraordinary minister* of Communion who is instituted permanently.[13] In case of genuine necessity, a simple faithful may be *appointed* by the bishop (or Vicar) as extraordinary minister of Holy Communion (the so-called *lay minister*). This appointment is always for a specific occasion or for a time. The lay minister should be duly instructed and distinguish himself by his Christian life, faith, and morals.[14]

---

[12] Code of Canon Law, c. 910.1.
[13] GIRM, no. 65; Code of Canon Law, c. 910.2.
[14] Paul VI, *Immensae Caritatis*.

35. Prayer after Communion

Lord, you gave them the food of angels, from heaven untiringly send-
ing them bread already prepared, containing every delight, satisfying
every taste (Wis 16:20).

After Communion, the priest returns to the altar and collects any
remaining particles. He purifies the paten or ciborium over the chalice, and then the chalice itself. In silence he prays:

Lord, may I receive these gifts in purity of heart.
May they bring me healing and strength, now and for ever.

Afterward, if circumstances allow it, the priest and the people may
spend some time in silent prayer. If desired, a hymn, psalm, or some
other song of praise may be sung by the entire congregation.[1]

On some days, during this period of silent prayer, we will find it
easy to tell our Lord how much we love him. At other times, however, we will feel as if God is hiding from us. In such moments, we
will have to advance like blind men feeling their way, like little
children learning to walk. Sometimes, it will be our own fault, even
though our mistakes may seem to us to be nothing at all. Our pride
then leads us to justify what has no justification. Perhaps the things
we have thought, said, or done are grave faults, all the graver the
closer we are to God. Perhaps, we may have lacked charity, and
have forgotten that to hurt one of God's children is to hurt God
himself.[2]

Then, standing at the altar or at the chair and facing the people,
the priest, with hands outstretched, says, "Let us pray." There may
be a brief period of silence, unless this has been already observed
immediately after Communion. The priest recites the Prayer after
Communion, at the end of which the people respond, "Amen."[3]

---

[1] GIRM, no. 56j.
[2] Bernard Vasconcelos, *Your Mass*, p. 130.
[3] GIRM, no. 122.

The greeting is now made real in its highest sense: the Lord *is* with us, with those who have received Communion.

IN THE Prayers after Communion, we find, once again, the characteristic features of the Roman Collects: a restrained style and an unobtrusive and quietly lyrical quality. They are often very well composed, indeed, and from them a theology of the effects of the Eucharist can be compiled: graces for the soul, an increase in the theological virtues, and in the gifts and fruits of the Holy Spirit; a remedy for the body; the unity of the Mystical Body; and eternal life. The expressions used ("bread of life," "life-giving food," "spiritual food," etc.) state formally the doctrine of the real presence of our Lord in the Eucharist.[4] Consider these examples:

Lord, may the power of your holy gifts free us from sin
and help us to please you in our daily lives.[5]

Keep us from our old and sinful ways and help us to continue a new life.[6]

Lord, we are nourished by the bread of life you give us.
May this mystery we now celebrate help us to reach eternal life with you.[7]

Help us to face the difficulties of the future with courage
and to give greater encouragement to our brothers in their present need.[8]

Lord, may the sacrifice we have offered strengthen our faith
and be seen in our love for one another.[9]

WE HAVE been nourished with the "bread of life," the food which is the source of our fortitude. This virtue of fortitude enables us to sustain the daily combat against our passions and weaknesses.

---

[4] F. Amiot, *History of the Mass* (New York: Hawthorn, 1959), p. 129.
[5] Saturday, fourth week of Lent.
[6] Friday, fourth week of Lent.
[7] Saturday after Ash Wednesday.
[8] Masses for Various Occasions and Needs; for Any Need.
[9] Thursday, second week of Lent.

According to the teachings of St. Thomas Aquinas, the virtue of fortitude is found in the man

- who is ready *aggredi pericula*, that is, "to face danger";

- who is ready *sustinere mala*, that is, "to put up with adversities for a just cause, for truth, for justice, and so on."

The virtue of fortitude goes hand in hand with the capacity of sacrificing oneself. This virtue had already a well defined contour among the ancients. With Christ it acquired an evangelical Christian contour. The Gospel is addressed to weak, poor, meek, and humble men, to peacemakers and to the merciful, but, at the same time, it contains a constant appeal to fortitude. The Gospel often repeats: "Fear not" (Mt 14:27). It teaches man that, for a just cause, for truth, for justice, one must be able to "lay down one's life" (Jn 15:13).

Allow me to draw your attention to examples that are generally not well known, but which bear witness in themselves to great, sometimes even heroic, virtue. I am thinking, for example, of a woman, already mother of a large family, who is "advised" by so many to suppress a new life conceived in her womb, by undergoing "the operation" of interruption of pregnancy; and she replies firmly: "no." She certainly feels all the difficulty that this "no" brings with it, difficulty for herself, for her husband, for the whole family, and yet she replies "no." The new human life conceived in her is a value too great, too "sacred," for her to be able to give in to such pressure.

Another example: a man who is promised freedom and also an easy career provided he denies his own principles, or approves of something that is against his sense of honesty toward others. And he, too, replies "no," though faced by threats on the one side, and attractions on the other. Here we have a courageous man!

Let us pray for this gift of the Holy Spirit which is called the "gift of fortitude." When a man lacks the strength to "transcend" himself, in view of higher values, such as truth, justice, vocation, faithfulness in marriage, this "gift from above" must make each of us a strong man and, at the right moment, say to us "deep down": Courage! [10]

We can profit a lot from the Prayers after Communion by using them as inspiration for personal reflection during the course of the day.

[10] John Paul II, *Courage!* (address at the General Audience of November 15, 1978).

PART V
CONCLUDING RITE AND PERSONAL THANKSGIVING

36. The Concluding Rite

"You are my witnesses. And now I am sending down to you what the Father has promised. Stay in the city. . . ." They worshiped him and then went back to Jerusalem full of joy (Lk 24:48–49, 52).

The Concluding Rite is quite simple. It includes the blessing, the dismissal, and the kissing of and reverence to the altar.

Once the Prayer after Communion is concluded, the priest greets us in the usual manner, extending his hands. As he receives our answer, he blesses us with these words:

May almighty God bless you,
the Father, and the Son, ✠ *and the Holy Spirit.*

"Amen," we answer.

On certain days or occasions, a more solemn form of blessing or prayer over the people may be used.

Then the priest gives us the sign of dismissal:

The Mass is ended, go in peace

or some other formula, such as:

Go in peace to love and serve the Lord.

We reply as always:

Thanks be to God.

The priest kisses the altar as at the beginning. Then he makes the proper reverence (a low bow—or a genuflection, if the Blessed Sacrament is there) with the ministers and leaves.

This part of the ceremony reveals the true character of the Mass. It is not a crowd watching a beautiful memorial service. It is the Church gathered around the altar, together with Christ her Head, who offers the sacrifice of the cross. Therefore, one should not think that anyone could come at any time, pray there as he fancies, and go away when he likes. We, therefore, stand while the priest and the ministers leave the sanctuary. We feel part of the Church and members of the Mystical Body of Christ.

The Mass is finished; we are encouraged to return to our ordinary occupations "to love and serve the Lord." We serve the Lord while fulfilling our usual norms of piety, resting, or working in the presence of God. In this way we constantly keep alive those dispositions we had during the Mass.

When the Lord was about to crown his work on earth, he asked his Father, "Keep those you have given me true to your name, so that they may be one like us. I am not asking you to remove them from the world, but to protect them from the evil one. They do not belong to the world any more than I belong to the world" (Jn 17:11, 15–16).

The Lord does not want us removed from our surroundings, our work, or our social relationships. He wants us in the world so that we might sanctify and improve it, and place at God's feet all souls and institutions, all political life and all activities in general.

Blessed Josemaría Escrivá points out for us, "Your ordinary contact with God takes place where your fellow men, your yearnings, your work and your affections are. There you have your daily encounter with Christ. It is in the midst of the most material things of the earth that we must sanctify ourselves, serving God and all mankind." [1]

Therefore the Mass should not be taken as a kind of escape from our duties. "Have no doubt: any kind of evasion from the honest realities of daily life is for you, men and women of the world, something opposed to the will of God." [2] On the contrary, we should turn to our daily occupations to find God also in these pursuits. Thus, we will avoid leading a double life: "on one side, an interior life, a life of relation with God; and on the other, a separate and distinct professional, social, and family life, full of small earthly realities.

"No! We cannot lead a double life. We cannot be like schizophrenics, if we want to be Christians. There is just one life, made of flesh and spirit. And it is this life which has to become, in both soul

---

[1] J. Escrivá de Balaguer, *Conversations*, no. 113.
[2] Escrivá, *Conversations*, no. 114.

and body, holy and filled with God. We discover the invisible God in the most visible and material things. There is no other way. Either we learn to find our Lord in ordinary, everyday life, or else we shall never find him." [3]

[3] MF, no. 59.

37. Personal Thanksgiving

Bless God, utter his praise before all the living for all the favors he has given you. Proclaim before all men the deeds of God as they deserve, and never tire of giving him thanks (Tob 16:6).

We leave the holy banquet of Communion as happy as the Three Wise Men would have been if they could have carried away the Child Jesus. "Simeon gave back Jesus to his Mother; he kept him in his arms only one moment. We are far happier than Simeon. We may keep him always if we will." [1] Lazarus often entertained our Lord in his home at Bethany. But in Communion, Jesus not only comes into our arms, or sits by our side, but also enters and dwells in our hearts. Thus, our heart ought to glow in the same way that the hearts of the disciples on the road to Emmaus burnt within them as Christ spoke and explained the Scriptures to them.

It is natural that we desire to remain a few minutes in prayer and thanksgiving after the Mass. The Church recommends this practice. [2] Sometimes, we will be talking with Christ. At other times, we will say nothing at all; we will simply look at him and he will look at us.

We should also know that Christ's body and blood remain in us after Communion *as long as the accidents of the bread and wine remain as such.* As soon as these accidents are changed by our bodily processes, Christ's real presence ceases to be. Nevertheless, we continue living in his Mystical Body.

While Christ is *physically* present inside us in the form of the consecrated species, we must be grateful and gracious hosts to him. For in a very tangible way, he has chosen to dwell in our body and make it his temple.

Pope Paul VI, in his encyclical *Mysterium Fidei*, referred to the reproach of

---

[1] Jean Marie Vianney (The Curé D'Ars), *Eucharistic Meditations*, Sermon of the Feast of the Purification.

[2] Sacred Congregation of the Rites, *Eucharisticum Mysterium*, no. 38.

Novatian, whose testimony is trustworthy in this matter. He felt that anybody deserved to be condemned who "came out after Sunday service bringing the Eucharist with him, as was the custom, . . . and carried the holy body of the Lord around with him," going off to places of amusement instead of going home.[3]

St. John tells us in his Gospel that "as soon as Judas had taken the piece of bread he went out. Night had fallen" (13:30). Often, no sooner has the priest left the altar than people start leaving the church, hastily. They are ready at once to converse with any person who will speak to them, except to Jesus Christ, who would have so many things to say to them, and so much good to do them. Where is their faith?

Blessed Josemaría Escrivá thus advises us: "Do not leave the church almost immediately after receiving the sacrament. Surely you have nothing so important to attend to that you cannot give our Lord ten minutes to say thanks. Let's not be mean. Love is paid for with love." [4]

It is true that on some days, we will not be able to remain in the church after Mass, because of some pressing task or duty. But couldn't we arrange things in such a way that we usually find time for our personal thanksgiving? It is a matter of giving due importance to it, and including it among the things that we want to do. For isn't it true that when we want to do something, we find time for it?

The content of our thanksgiving will be just a continuation of the sentiments and affections we have felt—or tried to foster in ourselves—during the Mass, but perhaps in an atmosphere of greater intimacy this time. Sometimes, acts of faith, hope, and charity addressed to the Three Divine Persons will spurt from our soul. At other times, we will maintain an intimate dialogue with Jesus, our divine Friend who will purify and transform us. Or perhaps, we will just be sitting still, in silent adoration, in the same manner that a mother watches over her son who has fallen asleep. According to St. Teresa, there is no other time than thanksgiving after Mass when we

---

[3] MF, no. 59.
[4] J. Escrivá de Balaguer, *A Priest Forever*, p. 19.

can so easily enrich our soul with virtues, or so rapidly advance to a high degree of perfection.

We should not look for prayers or formulas, if we do not find any need for them. But if we realize they can help us, we should overcome our laziness (say, to open our missal and read the prayers for thanksgiving there) or that subtle kind of vanity which makes us feel humiliated by having to read prayers composed by somebody else. We may, indeed, judge ourselves as having a degree of interior life so high that we can do without such prayers or formulas.

Have you tried to pray the *Trium Puerorum*, the song of the three young men (Dan 3:57ff.), inviting all creatures in heaven and on earth to join their hymn of thanksgiving?

> All things the Lord has made, bless the Lord.
> Angels of the Lord! all bless the Lord.
> Sun and moon! bless the Lord.
> Stars of heaven! bless the Lord.
> Showers and dews! all bless the Lord.
> Winds! all bless the Lord.
> Fire and heat! bless the Lord.
> Dews and sleet! bless the Lord.
> Light and darkness! bless the Lord.
> Lightning and clouds! bless the Lord.
> Mountains and hills! bless the Lord.
> Every thing that grows on the earth! bless the Lord.
> Let us praise and exalt him above all for ever.

A Final Prayer. We should remember to pray for all those who cannot be with us in this celebration because they do not share the faith of the Church. Here, we can be helped by the words of Pope Paul VI:

> May the most Blessed Virgin Mary, from whom Christ the Lord took the flesh that "is contained, offered, received" [5] in this sacrament under the appearances of bread and wine, and may all the saints of God and especially those who were

---

[5] Code of Canon Law, c. 897.

more inflamed with ardent devotion toward the divine Eucharist, intercede with the Father of mercies so that this common belief in the Eucharist and devotion to it may give rise among all Christians to a perfect unity of communion that will continue to flourish.[6]

Today, as yesterday, we face the evil—and the sad panorama—of disunity among Christians. What is the remedy, and where do we find the answer, to it? Where else but in the Eucharist. As the holy martyr St. Ignatius of Antioch exhorted us:

> Strive then to make use of one single thanksgiving. For there is only one flesh of our Lord Jesus Christ, and only one chalice unto the union of his blood, only one altar, only one bishop. . . .[7]

Jesus' Mother, who is also our Mother, gathers all her children at the foot of the cross of her Son. There she is, while our redemption is being accomplished:

> She cooperated, as the Second Vatican Council teaches, with maternal love. Here we perceive the real value of the words spoken by Jesus to his Mother at the hour of the cross: "Woman, behold your son" and to the disciple: "Behold your mother" (Jn 19:26–27). These are words which *determine Mary's place in the life of Christ's disciples* and they express the new motherhood of the Mother of the Redeemer: a spiritual motherhood, born from the heart of the Paschal Mystery of the Redeemer of the world.[8]

---

[6] MF, no. 75.
[7] *Epistle to the Philadelphians*, 4: PG 5:700.
[8] John Paul II, *Redemptoris Mater*, no. 44.

APPENDIX

38. Sacred Vessels and Vestments

O Lord, I love the house where you dwell, the place where your glory abides (Ps 25:8).

It is useful to know and to be able to identify the sacred vessels and liturgical items used in the cult, especially for the celebration of the Holy Mass.

Sacred vessels and liturgical items

The **altar** is the table on which the sacrifice of the Mass is offered. It must be covered with the altar cloths. There should be candles and a cross on the altar or somewhere not far from it.

The **reredos** or **altarpiece** is a richly painted or ornamented screen, usually with images, at the back of the altar.

The sacred books used in the Mass are called the **Lectionary**, which contains all the readings, psalms, and Gospels, and the **Sacramentary**. They are placed on the self-standing **lectern** for the readings or on a small folding **book stand** on the altar during the Mass.

The **tabernacle** is a boxlike receptacle where the Blessed Sacrament is reserved. It should be solid, inviolable, and located always in a place that is truly prominent and conducive to prayer. Its name is derived from the Latin word for "tent." It is covered with a **tabernacle veil**.

The **sanctuary lamp** must be kept burning before the tabernacle.

The **chalice** is a cup used at Mass to contain the precious blood of Christ.

The **paten** is a shallow dish on which the host is placed.

The **ciborium** is a covered cup in which the small consecrated hosts are kept. It is usually covered with a veil.

The **corporal** is a linen cloth, twenty inches square, upon which the chalice and paten are placed. It is pleated in three folds overlapping inwardly so that no fragment of the consecrated host may be dropped. It is carried in a **burse**.

The **pall** is a stiff cardboard, usually square, covered with linen. It is used as a cover for the chalice to protect it from dust and other foreign matter.

The **purificator** is a small linen towel used to dry the priest's fingers and the chalice at the end of the Mass.

The **chalice veil** covers the chalice before and after its use at Mass.

The **Communion plate** is held under the chin of the communicant to catch any particle of the sacred host that may fall. The **Communion cloth**, placed over the rail, has a similar purpose.

The **altar bell** is rung to alert those present at some moments of the Mass.

The **cruets** are two small bottles or vessels containing the wine and water to be used for the Consecration and for the ablutions after Communion.

In some places, it is customary to light a little candle on a **bougie lamp** during the Consecration.

A **censer** or **thurible** to burn incense is used in solemn Masses. The **incense boat** is a vessel in which incense is kept; a small spoon is used to transfer incense from the boat to the censer.

Priestly vestments

The **amice** is a rectangular piece of white linen, worn beneath the alb.

The **alb** is a full-length white linen vestment. It symbolizes the garment in which Christ was clothed by Herod, and the purity of soul with which the sacrifice of the Mass should be offered.

The **cincture** is a belt, girdle, or cord tied around the waist of the alb. It symbolizes chastity and mortification of the senses.

The **stole** is a long, narrow band worn over the neck. It symbolizes the sweet yoke of Jesus Christ and the dignity of the ministerial priesthood.

The **chasuble** is a sleeveless outer garment worn by the priest at Mass. It is worn over all the other vestments, and is made of silk or some other rich material usually decorated with symbols. It is patterned after the traveling cloak used by the ancient Greeks and Romans. Originally, it was a large circle of cloth with an opening in the center for the head of the priest. It symbolizes the charity which must cover all our actions.

At solemn Masses, the deacon wears a **dalmatic**. It is an outer liturgical vestment with short sleeves, open at the sides and made of the same material as the vestments of the celebrant.

The beauty of the vestments should derive from the materials and design rather than from lavish ornamentation. Representations on vestments should consist only of symbols, images, or pictures portraying the sacred. Anything not in keeping with the sacred is to be avoided.

The different **colors** of the liturgical vestments are meant to express the specific character of the mysteries of the faith being celebrated, to symbolize different truths, or to convey sentiments. Customarily, the color of these liturgical vestments (the chasuble, the dalmatic, the stole) is repeated in other items (the chalice veil, the tabernacle veil, the corporal burse, and even the frontal of the altar when it is made of cloth).

The color **white** is the symbol of purity, majesty, and glory. It is used on the feasts of our Lord, the Blessed Virgin, confessors, and virgins.

Red is the symbol of love, fire, the blood of martyrdom, and royalty. It is used on Palm Sunday, Good Friday, Pentecost, the Lord's Passion, and the feasts of the apostles, evangelists, and martyrs.

Green is the symbol of hope, youth, progress, life, and continuous growth. It is used in Masses of Ordinary Time.

Violet is the symbol of humility, penance, and austerity. It is used in Lent and Advent. It may also be used in Masses for the dead.

Black is the symbol of mourning. It may be used in Masses for the dead.

Rose lightens the austerity and penitential rigor of violet. It may be used on the Third Sunday of Advent and on the Fourth Sunday of Lent.

Light blue is the symbol of our Blessed Mother. It may be used on her feasts, following the regulations of the local bishop.

On solemn occasions more precious vestments may be used, even if not of the color of the day.[1]

---

[1] GIRM, nos. 306–309.

Index